N

FRONT LINE

Tom Dewar

Illustrations by Mary-Anne Bartlett

WOODTHORPE PUBLISHING
BRANCASTER STAITHE
NORFOLK

British Library Cataloguing in Publication Data. A catalogue record of this book is available from the British Library.

Published by: Woodthorpe Publishing,
Woodthorpe,
Brancaster Staithe,
King's Lynn,
Norfolk PE31 8BJ

Tel/Fax: 01485 210470

Printed by: Witley Press Ltd,
Hunstanton,
Norfolk PE36 6AD

Tel: 01485 532543
Fax: 01485 532715

ISBN 0 9520907 3 2

CONTENTS

ACKNOWLEDGEMENTS

There are certain people to whom I should like to offer special thanks, for without them it is improbable that this book would ever have seen the light of day: to R. A. N. Dixon, one time editor of the East Anglian Magazine, who first proposed the idea from which it finally developed; to my wife Ann Primrose, for her unwavering support, her patient reading and re-reading of the various drafts, her encouragement and always constructive suggestions; to Woodthorpe Publishing for discovering some merit in the stories, and in particular Maurice de Soissons, for his unstinted advice and guidance. Above all, my thanks must go to those fellow officers and men of The Royal Scots Fusiliers who, together with the hospitable people of Norfolk, provided the many and variegated threads from which these tales were woven.

Tom Dewar

FOREWORD

These stories seek to give some impression of what it was like to serve as a young army officer stationed in Norfolk during the years 1940 to 1942, when invasion by the enemy was a very real threat. Although they have the background of war, they are not strictly war stories in the normally accepted sense; there are no great tales of derring-do, no accounts of heroic deeds in battle. They concern the people of Norfolk as much as they do the soldiers who manned the defences.

All are based on actual incidents and events, although in some cases names have been changed to avoid any possibility of offence, embarrassment or distress being caused to individuals or to organisations.

1. WEYBOURNE

'He who would old England win,
Must at Weybourne Hope begin.'

Thus runs the ancient couplet. And once again, in 1940, Norfolk became a vital area in the defence of England. Sir F. H. Hinsley, more recently Master of St John's College, Cambridge, and closely involved in British Intelligence during the war, emphasised this when he wrote: 'the British planners assumed that the main assault would be made on East Anglia, the best direction from which to envelop London.'

So sudden had been the disaster in France that the coast was virtually unprotected. Few fortifications had been built since the erection of the Martello towers against the Napoleonic threat. The miracle of Dunkirk had brought back the British Expeditionary Force but not their arms and armour; and those units which composed the front line defence force on the Norfolk coast were sadly lacking in fire-power. Strange weapons, ammunition for which was in very short supply, were issued from long-forgotten stores. To guard the entire coastline was obviously impossible, so defence positions were sited at the most vulnerable points, manned and connected by patrols, with the remainder of the troops working on other defences or engaged in training, but immediately available for action. This meant that the soldiers were billeted in most of the towns and villages along or near the coast, occupying requisitioned hotels or houses, and mingling with those civilians who still remained in the area.

This was the situation when the 'junior subaltern' arrived in the late summer of 1940 with his battalion, The 11th Royal Scots Fusiliers. They were now, as their CO tried to impress upon them, 'in the very front line.' For them Churchill's words were much more than mere rhetoric. They might indeed have to fight on the beaches of Wells or Cromer or Sheringham: they might have to fight in the streets of Holt or

Blakeney; and they might have to die there. No soldier at that time doubted that the Germans would come, and they were well aware of their own defensive inadequacies. That was the reality, but one difficult to grasp for a 'civilian-soldier' finding himself in these particular surroundings on the Norfolk coast during those lovely summer days. All around him were the civilian conditions of life from which he had only recently been snatched: shops, offices, pubs open; people going about their daily business; pretty girls in summer frocks. Many things were of course different: empty houses, few children, little traffic, deserted sea and shore. But to the soldier there was little resemblance to the front line of battle as he had imagined it and for which he had been prepared.

It was strange, too, for those civilians who still remained in what was a restricted area. Barbed wire in their gardens, trenches on their golf courses, roads blocked, favourite picnic sites mined. They were prevented from enjoying the facilities of shore and sea. Fishermen and farmers, urged by the government to produce more food, often found their efforts frustrated by military requirements. There was some friction, but not much. Soldiers and civilians, together in the front line found a common sense of purpose. Many friendships were developed, many bonds forged between them.

These circumstances helped greatly to clarify the soldier's war. Involved as he quickly became with local people and places, the abstract idea of fighting for King and Country was replaced by a more tangible one. When the Germans came, the soldier would be fighting to protect the people in his immediate area, amongst whom he had been living, and who had made him welcome in their homes. He would be fighting on what had become his own little patch of England. He would be fighting to defend a local community of which he had become a part.

All these thoughts returned again to the junior subaltern, now promoted to senior citizen, as he stood once more on Weybourne Hope almost 50 years to the day when first he had come there with his platoon. The concrete pill-box which he had helped to build, and in which he had set up his Hotchkiss machine gun (a relic of the Boer War), was still there. Nearby lay a hollow, all that remained of the trench in which the home-made Molotov cocktails had been kept, the feeble weapons issued to them to defend this outpost against the might of the enemy. To his left, Muckleburgh Hill still stood solid, but scarred no longer by lines of trenches and barbed wire. Behind him were the outlines of the little flint cottages of Weybourne village, greatly changed but still recognisable. At his feet the grey North Sea, in one of its quieter moods, rumbled gently over the shingle. The Germans, thanks to the bravery of the pilots of the RAF, and to the strange decisions of their own High Command, had never come; but as he stood there on the Hope, so many memories came flooding back of people long ago and of events long past; reminders of those heady days of 1940, when Norfolk had served as the bastion of England.

2. GREAT YARMOUTH

The junior subaltern stood at the sand-bagged, unglazed window of the empty room, gazing over the dark outline of Wellington Pier. A small coaster was steaming its erratic course northwards through the calm sea, dragging behind it a thin plume of smoke and its protective barrage balloon, reminding him illogically of one of those comic postcards depicting an inebriated party-goer making his unsteady way home. Dusk was falling at the end of a day during which his introduction to East Anglia in general, and to Great Yarmouth in particular, had been both precipitate and perplexing.

Less than one week before, he and his battalion had been gently soldiering in the English shires, with his only worries being an inability to equate a subaltern's pay of 9s 6d with a compulsory mess bill of 10 shillings a day; and how to escape orderly officer duties on his imminent 21st birthday. He reflected on the momentous events of the past few days. The code word 'Cromwell' – signifying 'invasion imminent' – had shattered that life of comparative ease and luxury. The rôle of the battalion had changed immediately; within four days it had been transported to East Anglia to become part of a brigade defending the Norfolk coastline. "We are honoured and proud to be moving into the front line," the CO had told his assembled officers; a few of whom, only recently returned from France via Dunkirk, seemed rather less enthusiastic, with dark mutterings about the royal plural.

So it was that, early one morning in late summer, 1940, the junior subaltern and his platoon found themselves standing on the pavement on the sea front in Yarmouth, surrounded by an untidy heap of rifles, kit bags and the other paraphernalia, accoutrements and impedimenta of war. Across the street stood a three-storey building, on the ground floor of which was a small fish and chip shop. The name on the fascia had been blacked out, presumably for security reasons, though it occurred to him that whoever had ordered this must have a very low opinion of

German map-reading abilities. The shop was very obviously closed. This building, as the company commander had indicated, was to be the platoon's defensive strong point. His orders had been simple, brief and to the point. "That's yours," he said, pointing to the building; "get cracking." Orders not to be found in any military manual, but none the less effective. The company commander thereupon drove off in his truck at high speed, as was his wont, crashing the gears and startling a flock of pigeons feeding on the verge of the Aquarium Gardens.

The junior subaltern regarded 'his' building. He then looked at the rather motley crew of war-time soldiery who made up 11 Platoon, 11th RSF. These warriors were already taking the opportunity to fraternise with a group of young female citizens who had gathered to see what was happening. As he looked at his platoon, he pondered on what his immediate course of action should be. One lesson at least the army had taught him: when in doubt, 'brew-up'. One could hardly do this on a busy street in a town which, even if it were in the front line, was still thronged with people. He looked up and down the street, and found inspiration. Not far away was a sign, 'Café Open'. He turned to his platoon sergeant, that ever-present help in trouble, and gave him brief instructions and a pound note.

"Get fell in youse yins," shouted Sergeant Canning in a voice which startled the unfortunate pigeons once again, and which brought on a fit of giggles amongst the female bystanders. The command produced only a reluctant response from the soldiers, whose fraternising activities were obviously progressing favourably. Soon, however, having been exhorted by further suitable words from their sergeant, they were marched off towards the café, leaving behind two unfortunates detailed to guard the pile of equipment.

The junior subaltern looked across at the rather unpromising building which he had to convert into an anti-invasion stronghold against the might of the German army. "Ah well," he mused, "might as well have a recce." He walked across the street, and in through the unlocked door. Thus did he assume his first operational command in the front line: not heroically to the sound of shot and shell, not to the acrid smell of burning cordite, but in a rather more prosaic way, to the noise of a creaking café door, and the sour odour of stale cooking fat in a deserted fish and chip shop on the sea front in Great Yarmouth.

3. OFFICERS AND GENTLEMEN

The 11th Battalion Royal Scots Fusiliers, the 21st of Foot, was embodied at Melton Mowbray in the early summer of 1940. At first it acted as a holding battalion, being gradually trained and brought up to strength as a battalion of the line. Most of its members were war-time soldiers; the junior subaltern was himself one of the 'amateurs'. When war was declared in 1939, he had just completed his first year as an undergraduate at St John's College, Cambridge. Instead of returning to the university at the end of the long vacation, he, along with several of his contemporaries, enlisted in the army. For some reason best known to the War Office, they were all posted to The Worcestershire Regiment at Norton Barracks, an establishment ill-designed to withstand the harsh winter of 1939-40. After a few very uncomfortable months there, he was selected to attend an officers' training course at the OCTU in Bulford, thence to emerge with a commission in the 11th RSF.

In the battalion there was a small but very important nucleus of regular soldiers, who made up the senior elements. Outstanding amongst these was the commanding officer, Lieutenant-Colonel Walter Syfret, and the adjutant, later to become second-in-command and ultimately to command the battalion, A.R.W.C. Montgomery-Cunninghame. Theirs was the task of moulding the unit, which was receiving at regular intervals batches of raw recruits and young, inexperienced officers, into an efficient fighting force; a duty which they carried out with considerable success, even though with widely different methods. In only two aspects were they alike: each owned a baby Austin Seven, and each had a small dog as his constant companion. Sally, an Aberdeen terrier, and Jocky, a small Jack Russell, were as much a part of the battalion as any of its soldiers.

In everything else 'Wally' and 'Monty' (not to be confused with a more famous officer of the same name) were different. The CO was a

South African who had served with distinction in the 1914-18 War, as his many medal ribbons bore witness. He had settled in England, having transferred to the British Army. He had retired in the 1930s, but had been recalled to the RSF on the outbreak of hostilities. He was quietly efficient, gentle in speech and manner, sympathetic to the needs and to the difficulties of young and inexperienced officers whom the monthly intakes were introducing into his battalion.

Monty was very different. Comparatively young, perhaps in his late twenties, he was a regular officer to whom promotion had come rapidly because of the war. He was said to have the longest name on the Army List, and to be, at the height of six feet nine inches, one of the tallest officers. To see him disentangling himself from his immaculately kept baby Austin was something to be watched in disbelief; it seemed impossible that so small a car could accommodate such long legs. Monty was not impressed by 'amateur' soldiers. To him, they were a necessary evil, one that had to be endured because the battalion depended on them. He realised that he, as adjutant, must try to make them into efficient officers. Harsh words came frequently from his lips, praise seldom. He was feared but respected by all the junior ranks.

He was a firm believer in the value of ceremonial as a useful military discipline. With officers and men on defence duties, this was not easy to practise; but whenever possible a guard-mounting parade was held at battalion HQ, taken by the officer of the day. Monty kept a close watch on this, especially if the officer concerned was a very junior one. He insisted on the minutest detail being observed in procedure and in dress. Strict instructions were issued, one of these being that the orderly officer must arrive on the parade ground exactly five minutes before the guard mounting was due to begin. He must then march to and fro across the square, at a regular pace, until the RSM reported the guard ready for his inspection.

At Blakeney, the battalion HQ was in the Blakeney Hotel, on the quay side, with the officers' mess in a house called 'White Gables', about four minutes' march away. Orderly officers, aware of Monty's insistence on punctuality – it was, in his book, equally as heinous to be a minute early on parade as a minute late – would watch from one of the windows to see when Monty set out. They then left the mess themselves and, by taking a short cut through the grounds of the Manor Hotel, they could arrive on the parade ground outside Blakeney Hotel exactly on time, and just as Monty appeared. They would then march on to the parade ground together. This the junior subaltern, on his first time as orderly officer, was determined to do, even going so far as to time himself exactly over the route.

Guard mounting that day was detailed for 1700 hours – 5 pm. Correctly dressed, brasses shining, cane, gloves to hand, he watched from the window of his room which overlooked the front door, ready to leave as soon as he saw Monty appear. Suddenly he was horrified to see the tall figure of the adjutant at the corner of the drive, heading for the gate. Monty must have left by the back door, hidden from his sight. He was going to be late on parade.

He bounded down the stairs, out into the drive, and, taking the short cut, arrived on the Blakeney parade ground just as Monty was taking his first strides across the tarmac. Panting he fell into step. As they turned about smartly on the far side, the junior subaltern heard the fatal words. "Late on parade – report to me afterwards."

Monty, first as adjutant and then as second-in-command, did more than his share in moulding the battalion into the good unit which it undoubtedly became. Later in the war he became commanding officer of the battalion, and lost his life leading it into battle in France. As one of his friends said, when bullets were flying, Monty's extra inches were something of a disadvantage.

Captain Cruden, another regular officer who had enjoyed accelerated promotion, was one who managed to circumvent regulations regarding the presence of officers' wives. Newly married, he rented the windmill at Cley-next-the-Sea for several months. The Crudens were hospitable by nature, and the converted windmill was the scene of many good parties. They managed to persuade the signals officer to lay a telephone line from their home to C Company HQ, so that Captain Cruden could be summoned back in case of emergency. He also maintained that, because of the position of the windmill, he had a perfect view over the marshes and out to sea, and thus was better placed to avoid surprise by the enemy than in his proper battle post. Unfortunately, he was somewhat eccentric in behaviour as an officer, and his stay with the battalion was a comparatively brief one.

Captain Bill Smith was B Company commander, and as such was the junior subaltern's immediate superior. Socially, he was good fun; on parade and militarily, he was strict. Few words of praise passed his lips. He expected his officers to behave properly, and to carry out their duties efficiently. If they failed to come up to the high standard that he set, he was not slow to voice his displeasure. He disclosed little about his private life. By profession he was a lawyer, and it was generally understood that he had recently been divorced.

Some time after the move to Norfolk the junior subaltern was flattered to be asked to a celebratory dinner, just the two of them, at the Duke's Head in King's Lynn. This was outside their district, but one of the occasional, and rare, 24-hour company stand-downs was due shortly, so they could go outside their area without disobeying regulations.

On the arranged day, the two of them left Sheringham in Captain Smith's old baby Austin (one of three now in the battalion) on the 40-mile journey to King's Lynn. The company commander fancied himself as a driver, and they rattled along at a good pace. On approaching their destination, they slowed down; the driver had something to say. He hadn't, he explained, been quite open about the evening. He had arranged to meet a certain lady at the Duke's Head, a lady of whom he was particularly fond, a divorcée. He didn't want this publicly known. There was a complication: she had a teenage daughter with her. He would be greatly obliged if the junior subaltern would entertain the daughter somewhere out of the way, a café meal perhaps, then the pictures: he would gladly stand the expense incurred.

A junior officer, if he is wise, does not refuse a request made by his senior. In the lounge of the Duke's Head they met the lady concerned and her young daughter. After introductions had been made, and some polite conversation, the captain indicated that the time had come for the party to divide. It was obvious that the daughter had also received her instructions, for she seemed quite happy to accompany her escort out into the evening and King's Lynn market place. A nearby cinema incorporated a modest restaurant in which they ate before going in to watch the film: the sum of money proffered by the captain was sufficient to cover this, and an ice cream at the interval.

On their return to the hotel they found their elders enjoying drinks by the fire in the lounge. The evening must have gone well, for an additional whisky was ordered and the junior subaltern was invited to join them, the daughter having been instructed to go up to bed. Several more drinks were consumed, and by about 11.30 pm when it was time to leave, the captain was in a merry mood; he had certainly been celebrating well. The junior subaltern tactfully made his way out to the car to allow the other two privacy for their leave taking. Some 10 minutes later, Captain Smith appeared; his passenger wondered if he were in a fit state to drive, but of course dared not voice his doubts. His fears, in any event, were needless. The car had moved only a few yards down the street when the engine, having previously issued some alarming sounds, ground to a halt. The captain spent some minutes beneath the bonnet attempting to rectify matters, but in vain. The car had evidently decided that it was not going to move again that night.

The two men returned to the hotel just before the front doors closed. Telephone calls to various taxi firms were unavailing. In those days of petrol rationing, no drivers were willing to expend the amounts of precious fuel needed for such a journey. Matters were becoming serious. Failure to return to Sheringham by 7 am could lead to a charge of being absent without leave. There was only one thing left to do. Captain Smith telephoned the duty officer at Battalion HQ, fortunately on this occasion a fellow officer in his own B Company. He told him to get the company driver, Fusilier Hickman, out of bed and instruct him to come to collect them in the PU 8 hundredweight (pick-up) van, as quickly as possible. It was against regulations for army transport to be used for recreational purposes, so the duty officer was to keep his mouth shut. Hickman wouldn't like losing his night's sleep, but that couldn't be helped.

The call completed, the two officers returned to the lounge with a half bottle of Black Label, extracted from the porter at a wickedly high price, and there awaited the arrival of their transport. By the time a still indignant Hickman had arrived, the captain had made considerable inroads into the bottle. His companion had preferred to snooze by the fire. The captain had a few words with his driver, and a couple of pound notes were transferred after which the latter, now in better mood, led them out to the PU.

It was with no little sense of relief that the junior subaltern later made his somewhat stiff way up to his room in the mess. It had been a cold and uncomfortable journey in the back of the vehicle. The captain, more comfortably seated in the front, and sustained by an occasional dram from his hip flask into which he had transferred the remainder of the whisky, had less cause to complain. His consumption of alcohol during the evening and night had been considerable, but he seemed little affected.

There was just time for a quick bath, a shave, a change into battledress and a welcome cup of gunfire tea provided by an anxious Percival, his batman, before the junior subaltern hurried to the parade ground, the former carpark of the Sheringham Hotel, where he joined his fellow officers lined up behind their company commander. On the command, "Fall in, the officers" they all took their places in front of their respective platoons. Captain Smith's capacity for holding his drink had earlier impressed his companion; but now the cold, fresh morning air was exerting its influence. The captain was seen to be swaying gently before his assembled company, whose members were all standing rigidly to attention, straight as ramrods, in perfect parade formation. A scowl creased the company commander's brow, as he continued to sway slowly and unwittingly from side to side. "Stand still, you men," he roared in his best parade-ground voice, "stand STILL!" He glared again at his well-disciplined ranks of soldiery. The junior subaltern feared what might happen next. Fortunately, the effect of the fresh air and alcohol combination must have worn off quickly, for the captain ceased to sway, and had regained the perpendicular. "That's better, men" he roared. "Fall out, the officers: carry on, sergeant major."

The final crisis of a long and eventful celebratory evening had staggered at last to a satisfactory conclusion.

4. FLYING PICKET

The idea of a mobile force, capable of engaging at short notice any parachutists dropped by the enemy behind the main coastal defences, was no doubt a sound one. The method adopted was less convincing. Motorised transport was in short supply; most of the army's vehicles had been left behind in France. And so, instead of scout cars and motor cycles, the mobile force was allocated thirty army-type pedal bicycles. The personnel for this new flying picket was to be provided by whichever battalion happened to be holding the reserve position in and around Gresham's School at Holt.

11th RSF were in reserve when the plan came into effect, and B Company was ordered to supply one platoon for this purpose. On company parade, Captain Smith asked for volunteers. The men of 11 Platoon, no doubt seeing a chance to escape further route marches, disregarded their normal custom never to volunteer for anything, and raised their hands to a man. They thus became brigade flying picket, with the junior subaltern as its reluctant commander.

He was faced with several immediate difficulties. As he had suspected, a number of his men lacked a very basic qualification: they had never in their lives ridden a bicycle. These were assigned to maintenance duties. The cycles themselves were heavy, clumsy, grey, lumbering machines which had no doubt been lying for years in some long-forgotten stores. The manual of bicycle drill accompanying them had been published in 1911. The machines had no handbrakes; braking was achieved by back-pedalling; there was no method of free-wheeling, which made progress on a downhill slope a hazardous procedure for those accustomed to more modern machines.

Once the cycles had been collected from Holt station, much to the relief of the stationmaster, and the layers of thick protective grease had been removed by the non-cyclists (now regretting their earlier enthusiasm), the picket commander held his first cycle parade. It was

... and the foggy silence of early morning was shattered by the sound of crashing bicycles...

not an unqualified success; in fact Captain Smith, an interested spectator, made later reference to disorganised chaos and, later still, kept his friends in the bar of The Feathers in fits of laughter as he described the scene. The junior subaltern decided to abandon the complexities of the manual and to depend thereafter on simplicity. Things improved. After further practice around the school grounds, and the elimination of a few chronic waverers, coordination was more or less achieved between men and machines, and it was decided, not without misgivings, to risk taking to the public highway.

Early one morning, so as not to interfere with normal duties, the flying picket formed up in its three columns and, with its commander at the head, negotiated the school gates without mishap and swung right towards the town. A thick mist covered Holt; this became denser as they reached the main street, but the junior subaltern, relieved that their progress was shrouded from the eyes of the locals, with growing confidence increased the pace. Then, forgotten by the picket leader, out of the fog loomed the Jubilee Memorial directly in their path.

The junior subaltern took swift evasive action to his left, followed by the middle column. Collision with the left hand section, who had no time to react, was inevitable, and the foggy silence of early morning was shattered by the sound of crashing bicycles and the unprintable oaths of their riders. The citizens of Holt can seldom have had such a rude awakening (there may still be some who can recall that morning). The right hand column missed the obstruction and continued on its now leaderless way. The first incline of Letheringsett Hill was upon them. Unable to free-wheel, inexpert in the art of back-pedalling, with increasing speed they began to descend the hill which would eventually lead them to the bridge over the River Glaven and inevitable disaster; but happy chance intervened. Unable to see the curve in the road, so thick had become the fog, the whole column of eight cyclists failed to negotiate the bend, and instead headed straight on through the rectory gates, to end up in a tangled heap of men and machines in the shrubbery which lined the drive. The ensuing clamour awoke Canon King, who was not amused. It was a bedraggled group of men who wheeled their damaged cycles back to Gresham's.

Having made the necessary repairs, and an apology delivered to the rector, the platoon resumed its practice drill, and at last became efficient enough to merit the approval of the brigadier, who took the salute from the steps of the school cricket pavilion as the flying picket achieved a somewhat shaky 'cycle-past'. Now, under the new name of 'flying column', they were reinforced by three strange, lumbering armoured vehicles called Armadillos. These remarkable machines were so difficult to start, and so slow once they had got under way, that on practice schemes they were left far in arrears of the cyclists. Indeed, they spent much of their time immobile, parked sadly alongside the school chapel.

Only once was the flying column called out in earnest, when a report was received that enemy parachutists had been seen landing near Bodham Street. It was already dusk, and the army had provided only two cycle lamps, one for the commander at the front, and one red lamp for the platoon sergeant at the rear. However, they set off at a good speed, excited by the thoughts of real action, the Armadillos waddling far behind. Then, at the Kelling road junction, their progress was halted by a policeman standing in their way, waving his torch. The junior subaltern having ordered 'halt' and 'dismount', approached the constable, expecting to be given further information about the parachutists. He was somewhat surprised therefore to be asked instead why they were cycling without lights after lighting-up time. In vain did he explain the urgency of their mission. Apparently the law was the law. Out came the notebook: all their names would be taken, and without lights they would not proceed further. The picket commander, reluctantly left with no alternative but to order the physical removal of this staunch upholder of the law, was saved from this embarrassment in the nick of time by the arrival of a motor cyclist from HQ bearing the news that the report of the enemy landing was erroneous. The parachutists had been the crew of an RAF bomber baling out of their damaged plane.

Once again, this time escorted by the constable still adamant about lights, they pushed their cycles back to base, where they found that one of the Armadillos had managed to get itself wedged in the school gates, effectively blocking the entrance. A few days later orders came through disbanding the flying column. It was with some relief that the junior subaltern and 11 Platoon returned the cycles to store, and resumed their less glamorous pedestrian duties.

5. ROCKET HOUSE

A narrow track leads through the saltmarshes which lie between the village of Salthouse and the sea. At the end of this path there once stood, on a rocky outcrop, a building known locally as Rocket House. Today, victim of time and tide, it is there no longer, but in 1940, although reduced to a ruin, its remaining walls were stout enough to be incorporated in a strong defensive post.

One night in February, 1941, the junior subaltern set out with his small patrol to visit the section on duty at Rocket House. It was a vile night. A north-easterly gale was blowing, carrying with it vicious hail showers which stung and cut any exposed flesh. The only consolation was the thought that no German in his right mind would attempt a landing in such conditions.

When they reached Rocket House they found that the tide was especially high, and the post had become an island. The patrol was already soaked to the skin, so the final splashing through the icy sea made little difference to its discomfort. After an exchange of passwords, the junior subaltern went into the post, leaving the remainder of the patrol to shelter behind the ruins. On entering, he was surprised to find Corporal Simpson, a reliable and normally unflappable NCO, in an unusually excited state, and to see that the entire section was awake. Normally, all except the duty sentries would be clustered round the coke stove, sound asleep. The corporal explained the reason. He had been roused by the sentries, who had reported that there was a dog howling outside. They had called to it, but no dog had appeared, and they could see nothing in the atrocious conditions. The corporal and the newly-awakened others had also heard a dog's howling and baying: "b…y scarey," said one man. The sounds had ceased just before the patrol's arrival.

The junior subaltern dismissed their concern and fears by suggesting that the sounds had been made by sudden squalls of wind blowing through the chinks and crannies of the ancient stonework. Further to reassure them, he took his unwilling patrol round the perimeter: traces of any animal there were none.

The story of Corporal Simpson's imaginary dog spread rapidly, losing nothing in the telling; and when his next tour of duty came round a few days later, he and his section departed down the track to Rocket House to the accompaniment of loud, dog-like noises and would-be witty comments from their mates working on the Salthouse village defences. The weather had made a sudden change for the better, and when the junior subaltern led out his patrol it was into a clear night, crisp with frost. Mist rising from the marshes glistened in the light of a full moon. Unusually for Salthouse, there was scarcely a breath of wind. When the patrol reached Rocket House the tide was at full ebb, so the men were able to cross the short stretch of sand dry-shod.

Once again the patrol commander found Corporal Simpson and his men in a state of excitement. The corporal himself had been on sentry duty at the machine gun embrasure. Suddenly, so he said, he heard loud baying and howling outside the post. Looking to his left towards Cley he had seen clearly in the bright moonlight a large, black dog bounding along the very edge of the sea. The dog, he continued, had stopped for a second, had then turned and rushed straight towards the place where he was standing, snarling as it came. On reaching the wall, the beast had reared on its hind legs and, with front paws against the stonework and straddling the Bren gun opening, had thrust its head towards the corporal inside. Startled, the corporal had drawn back, shouting to arouse the others. As he did so, he swung the gun on its mounting. The gun had struck the dog sharply on its muzzle and the animal, howling in pain, had disappeared from sight. The others, rushing to the look-out points, had seen no sign of the dog; the moon had been temporarily obscured by a passing cloud.

This time there was no wind to provide a possible explanation for the noise, and the junior subaltern was about to comment on the too vivid imagination of the corporal – it was not uncommon for sentries to become prey to their imaginations and to convert empty shadows into menacing realities – when he was diverted by a shout from outside. One of the patrol had found very distinct pawmarks imprinted on the firm sand. These were especially deep outside the embrasure at which Corporal Simpson had been standing. As the others crowded round this area, he followed the tracks in the sand. These appeared to lead directly out of the sea to Rocket House, circle it, then return straight back to the sea again. There were no impressions to the left or right, and none leading inland. He wondered greatly about this, but supposed that any lateral tracks must have been obliterated by the rapidly incoming tide. He could only surmise that the marks had been left by some stray dog which was hanging about in the hope of spare scraps of food; the troops often tried to 'adopt' such animals. A few days later, Corporal Simpson and another NCO, Sergeant Richardson, were posted to OCTU on an officers' training course, and left the battalion. The junior subaltern, with more important things on his mind, soon forgot these incidents.

Forgot them, indeed, until some eight years later when, the war over, he was browsing through the shelves of a second-hand bookshop in Cambridge. There, he chanced upon a book written by W. A. Dutt — 'The Highways and Byways of East Anglia'. From it he learned for the first time of the old superstition about Black Shug, sometimes known as Moggy Doo: the great, black, ferocious one-eyed dog said to roam the marshes of Norfolk by night; a dog whose footfall was completely silent, but whose roar could be heard above the noise of any storm. A dog whose eye was so evil that any person on whom it was cast was doomed to die a violent death within six months. The story at once reminded the ex-junior subaltern of Rocket House, and he wondered idly what Corporal Simpson was now doing, presuming he had survived the war.

The very next day he was at Grange Road, watching the 'Varsity XV playing against Bedford. To his surprise he found that the spectator standing beside him was the former Sergeant Richardson who had gone off to OCTU with Corporal Simpson all those years before, and neither of whom he had heard of, nor seen, since then. Back in his rooms in St John's after the match, he and the ex-sergeant sat by a precious coal fire, drinking tea and talking over old times. "You'll remember Corporal Simpson?" said Richardson. "You know, he was convinced that he had seen that dog at Salthouse, and was upset because you didn't seem to believe him. Said he didn't dare tell you it had only one eye, a great, blood-shot one."

"Too much imagination," replied the ex-junior subaltern; still, I expect he became a good officer. Any idea what happened to him after Bulford?"

"Oh, didn't you know?" said the ex-sergeant. "On the last day of the OCTU course, Simpson was on the battle range. The grenade he was holding went off prematurely in his hand – faulty fuse. Blew him into lots of little pieces."

6. CROMER CRABS

Here and there along the north Norfolk coast are gaps in the escarpment in which stand huddles of small buildings: cafés, ice-cream kiosks, souvenir shops. Here too, the fishermen keep their boats and other gear, with huts from which to sell some of their catch to holiday-makers during the season. These gaps are usually close to the main coastal highway, to which they are connected by minor roads. In 1940, when invasion threatened, they were considered to be defensively vulnerable; access to them by civilians was prohibited, and the approach roads were blocked and mined. Those who suffered most were obviously the fishermen, cut off as they were from their main source of livelihood.

Such a gap exists at East Runton. When the junior subaltern moved there with his platoon, his company commander was approached by a deputation from the fishermen. After listening with sympathy to their complaints, he replied that, officially he could do nothing; he was bound by orders from above. Unofficially, however, he was prepared to relax the prohibition, but the fishermen must observe certain conditions. They must always be led in and out by the junior subaltern, who alone knew the safety zones. No word of this arrangement must leak out else he, the company commander, would be in trouble. The fishermen readily agreed. The arrangements worked well. Lobsters and crabs – unrationed but expensive – began to appear on the slabs of local fishmongers for the first time for many months.

The officers of B Company stationed at East Runton were billeted in what, pre-war, had been a small guest-house, the Rose Hotel, a pleasant building tucked in behind the main street. The junior subaltern, much to his dismay, had been made the company messing officer. Army rations were adequate, but greatly lacking in variety, and he was expected to supplement these with something more acceptable. All five officers contributed two shillings per week to the 'kitty', upon which the junior subaltern could draw; and they expected to see results. Most food in the local shops was rationed, and of course he had no coupons at his disposal, so obtaining extras was not easy. During his first two weeks of office, his attempts to improve the menus was considered to be less than satisfactory; several disparaging remarks were directed his way.

Then, one Friday evening, his popularity increased suddenly and dramatically when a generous lobster salad appeared at the evening meal, to be followed on Monday by an equally delicious crab concoction. Shellfish of various sorts now became regular items on the menu, as did dabs, flounders and other fish dishes. Visits to the company mess by officers from other companies, and indeed from the CO and the adjutant, became embarrassingly frequent. Even the brigadier invited himself to dinner from his HQ near Norwich; there was just time to ensure that the gap was securely closed, and that nothing untoward was happening when he arrived.

Fellow officers knew that the weekly 'kitty' was quite insufficient to meet the cost of all this gastronomic excellence, but the junior subaltern declined to reveal the source fearing that, should word get about, higher authority would get to know about the arrangements made with the fishermen, with unfortunate repercussions. The source, should the truth be told, had a very simple explanation. The wife of one of the fishermen, grateful for the concessions granted to her husband, had approached the junior subaltern one day in the village. She had expressed her thanks, and had asked if he and his fellow officers would accept, as a token of her gratitude, a lobster salad for their evening meal. She would make this up herself and hand it in to the mess corporal after her husband's next catch. The junior subaltern accepted her offer with alacrity. Then, after the obvious success of this gift, he visited his benefactor to see if they could come to some financial arrangement for future supplies. Agreement was swift: one shilling for every crab or lobster salad, made up, and sufficient for five persons; other fish, as available, at similar cost.

The junior subaltern disclosed none of this, and the officers, happy with the situation, did not press him. Only two others knew the true facts; neither, for personal reasons, was likely to reveal them. The fisherman's wife would do nothing which might harm her husband's livelihood; the mess corporal was unlikely to do or say anything for fear of losing a valuable source of 'cook's perks'. And so B Company officers' mess continued happily to enjoy their varied and substantial meals, whilst the junior subaltern basked in the praise of his fellow officers and in the envy of other, less well-fed acquaintances.

Although enjoying his success as messing officer the junior subaltern had one small cloud on his conscience. One evening, after an especially good meal, Captain Smith, his company commander, made a comment which troubled him slightly. "Don't you think, " he asked, drawing noisily but happily on the filthy pipe which he always produced after the evening meal, "don't you think these fishermen might have shown some appreciation for what I've done for them? Bottle of Scotch, or something? A bit off, don't you think? Ah, well, why bother. As they say, there's a war on."

During his short time in the army, the junior subaltern had learnt much more than the basic lessons contained in training manuals. On return from his next leave, he brought with him a tin of Balkan Sobranie, the company commander's favourite tobacco. A few days later, he handed this to Captain Smith, giving the impression that it had been donated by the local fishermen in appreciation for what had been done for them. He was delighted; the other members of the mess, who had to endure the evening clouds of tobacco smoke, were less appreciative.

At the end of that month the regular change-over took place. B Company moved into reserve with the rest of the battalion in Holt, bringing the junior subaltern's messing duties to an end. Relieved of this responsibility, he thoroughly enjoyed his first dinner in the battalion officers' mess, set in the comfortable surrounding of the sanatorium of Gresham's School, his reputation untarnished and his conscience clear.

7. STYMIED AT SHERINGHAM

Included in the defences around Sheringham was the golf club. On various parts of the course pillboxes had been built, and some of the fairways near the cliff top had been mined and surrounded by wire. Anti-tank scaffolding was being erected alongside the railway track, and beside the main coast road. The course itself was a prohibited area, although members still had access to the club house, which they used for some social events.

One defence post, protected by a minefield, was in the area of Robin Friend. It was not permanently manned, but was patrolled and checked regularly. Danger notices were prominently displayed. Very early one morning in autumn the junior subaltern, on his tour of inspection, came over the rise on the fairway, and was surprised to see a man lying on the grass alongside the wire which surrounded the minefield. In his hand was a walking stick. This he had thrust through the entanglements, and was swinging to and fro close to the ground. Beside him stood a small white dog, barking excitedly.

On being challenged, the man stood up, dropping the stick. The junior subaltern recognised him as being a member of the staff of the Dormy Hotel, where he and his fellow officers had enjoyed many enjoyable off-duty evenings. In answer to his enquiries, the man explained that he was only collecting mushrooms, a practice of his for many years past. "Now," he complained, with much indignation, "now your damned wire is in the way." He further explained that he had been knocking off the mushroom heads with the stick handle; his dog then wriggled through a gap which he had made in the wire, and fetched out the mushrooms one by one. As a member of the golf club he was entitled to collect mushrooms on the course, even if the army had prevented his playing golf.

The junior subaltern, indicating the nearby warning notice, pointed out the dangers of such a practice. He also reminded the man that, in any case, he was in a prohibited area, golf club member or not, and requested him not to attempt it again. They then walked back to the town, where they parted amicably enough.

Thereafter, for several weeks, B Company officers enjoyed grilled mushrooms for their breakfast, mushrooms collected by the junior subaltern on his morning or evening patrols. Having himself helped in the laying of the minefields, he knew the safety lanes; he knew also that the mines were anti-tank and not anti-personnel and so, even if stood on, were unlikely to detonate under the weight of a man – or a dog. This fact he had considered neither necessary nor prudent to disclose to the intruder. However, further to cement military and civilian relationships, he did leave an occasional basket of mushrooms on the table of the hotel kitchen, until, autumn giving way to winter, mushrooms no longer flourished on the fairway at Robin Friend.

The junior subaltern was also involved in a further incident which concerned the Sheringham Golf Club and its members. Shortly after the mushroom episode, he, and several other army officers from the brigade were sent on a short liaison course with the RAF at West Raynham. The real object of this course was to try to repair the damage done to inter-service relationships at the time of Dunkirk, when the army felt that they had received inadequate protection from the RAF whilst the latter, in their turn, maintained that the army's performance in France had been less than impressive.

The army officers were made most welcome at West Raynham. They thoroughly enjoyed the hospitality offered them in the comforts of the station officers' mess, which contrasted greatly with the rather spartan conditions under which they had been living on the coast. At that time West Raynham was a base for Blenheims and Bostons, and the army officers were taken up for flights in these aircraft on several occasions. They were assured that, should any enemy aircraft be reported to be in the vicinity, the RAF 'planes would return immediately to base; not to protect army skins, but because they were unarmed, the guests having taken the place of RAF gunners. Nevertheless, it was always with some feeling of trepidation that the junior subaltern signed the 'blood-chit' before going up; this was a certificate absolving the RAF of any responsibility in the event of injury or death.

One day the junior subaltern was installed in the bomb-bay of a Boston, having previously been given a crash course on bombing techniques. The aircraft had been loaded with small practice bombs containing a quantity of flour. The target, selected by the junior

... the 'plane was now circling low over the golf clubhouse, the roof of which was liberally coated in white.

subaltern himself, was to be his company HQ, then established in the Grand Hotel on the sea front in Sheringham: a prominent building which should provide an easy target, and some good laughs on his return.

The outward flight over Norfolk and out over the North Sea was at a height which gave the junior subaltern a breathtaking panoramic view from his cramped position in his perspex cubby-hole. Then the aircraft turned back towards the coast, dropping as it did so to nought feet. As they flew just above the waves the impression of speed was exhilarating. The coastline came rapidly into view. The voice of the pilot on the intercom rang in his ears: "Target ahead!" The Grand Hotel loomed large. Trying to remember his instructions, the junior subaltern aligned his bomb sight. "On target!" He released his stick of bombs. "Bombs away!" The plane climbed rapidly, then swung on a wide curve and returned at a more leisurely speed to observe results.

The junior subaltern had had joyous visions of an irate company commander out on the promenade shaking his fist at the offending aircraft, perhaps even covered in flour; but that was not to be. No Captain Smith; indeed, no tell-tale white flour mark on the hotel roof or anywhere around it. The pilot's laugh crackled over the intercom. "Well, you hit something anyhow – look down to your right!" The 'plane was now circling low over the golf clubhouse, the roof of which was liberally coated in white. Outside, on the lawn, were a few angry-looking figures, gazing up at the aircraft and waving their arms furiously. As the 'plane headed back towards West Raynham, the pilot remarked, still obviously amused, "You were only about half a mile out; not too bad for a beginner – but I think I'll stick to my regular crew for ops!"

A few days later, the course completed, the junior subaltern returned to his army duties. On his first evening back, the battalion was holding an official mess night, to which some of the local dignitaries had been invited. It was the turn of the junior subaltern to be vice-president, seated at one end of the long table, with a guest on each side of him. During the course of the conversation the subject of service coordination came up. The guest on his right seemed to have strong views on the subject. "Navy man myself, ye know, in the last show – never had much time for these flying fellers – Brylcreme boys, no tradition, no manners. D'ye know, only the other day one of these damned idiots flew over the clubhouse and dropped sacks of flour all over the place. Beastly stuff came through the window – ruined our bridge club afternoon. Silly fools: time they grew up! Good mind to tell the war house – not that anyone there would listen!"

The junior subaltern, appalled by the sudden revelation that his chief guest had been the recipient of one of his misdirected flour bombs, was saved from any need to comment by the voice of the president calling down the table: "Mr Vice – if you please – The King!" It was with more than a little relief that the junior subaltern brought his fellow officers and the guests to their feet to drink the loyal toast, and summoned the pipe major, whose powerful lungs rendered further conversation unnecessary, indeed quite impossible, for the next 10 minutes. During this period the vice-president ensured that the port decanters circulated freely, and that the glass of his chief guest was frequently replenished. By the time that the pipe major had concluded his rendering of Highland airs, had accepted and disposed at one gulp the dram proffered, as is the custom, by the CO, and with much noisy stamping of feet had departed the mess, the senior member of the Sheringham Golf Club, RN retired, had become nicely mellowed, and had obviously forgotten the subject which had been under discussion. The junior subaltern, recklessly disregarding his current mess bill, ordered the mess corporal to bring a box of the best cigars, and led the conversation on to safer ground.

8. SANDRINGHAM'S MOVING GOALPOSTS

Coincidental with the battalion's move from Melton Mowbray to the Norfolk coast came orders from on high that all officers must set an example to their men in the matter of physical fitness. The CO of the 11th RSF responded to this dictum by deciding that all battalion officers when in reserve, and not on front line duties, must go for a daily pre-breakfast run of at least two miles.

This order must have come as a crushing blow to the battalion second-in-command, a stout, elderly regular major whose only apparent exertions hitherto had been to act as president of the mess committee, and to ensure that the two best armchairs were strictly reserved for the CO and himself; from lunch time onwards he usually made full use of his own chair. The only time that the junior subaltern had noticed any sign of liveliness was when the major had become incensed over the amounts of Stilton cheese which were being consumed – Melton Mowbray being, of course, noted for such a delicacy – and had drawn up a list which rationed each officer's Stilton allowance strictly according to rank. The second lieutenants, at the bottom of the list, with great daring petitioned the mess committee that therefore their mess bill should be accordingly reduced. Their petition was refused; they remained cheeseless and impecunious.

After the order had been given for the compulsory exercise, the appearance of the major on the running track was eagerly anticipated by the junior ranks: but they were to be disappointed. The major went immediately on leave, from which he never returned. Later, it was announced in Part II orders that he had been promoted, and had taken over as commandant of the base depot where, presumably, he was safe from undue physical demands.

The CO appointed a sports officer, whose task it was to arrange as many sporting fixtures as possible, subject always to the demands of the battalion's defensive duties and to military training. One of his first actions was to arrange a football match against the Leicesters; the game would be played on the town ground in Sheringham, where the Leicesters were then stationed. The RSF team was captained by the MT sergeant, in peace-time a professional player with Partick Thistle; the junior subaltern, with somewhat lesser qualifications (there was nobody else available), was selected to play in goal.

It would seem that to get lost on the short journey between Holt and Sheringham should be well-nigh impossible; but the RSF team succeeded in doing just that. It must, however, be remembered that the battalion had only very recently arrived in the area. Moreover, the sign posts on all roads had been removed for security reasons, and the roads were very much different from those of today. The team captain, the MT sergeant, who was also driving the truck, said he knew the way, and no map was required. One false turn had taken them into the maze of unsignposted lanes which lie between East and West Beckham and the coast. Many of the lanes were single track; some petered out completely, and the 3-ton truck was not easily manoeuvred. There was nobody about from whom to ask directions. They tried to keep heading northwards, knowing they must come eventually upon the coast road, but the Norfolk lanes refused to cooperate. At last they reached the A48 (which they should never have left in the first place) and arrived at Sheringham half an hour after the arranged kick-off time. They hurriedly took the field, their captain having previously instructed his team, on pain of seven days' jankers, never to mention the fact that they had got lost; the official explanation, a mechanical breakdown. The junior subaltern, although the only officer in the party, was quite happy to be ignored in all these proceedings, leaving everything to his captain, as every good team member should.

The RSF thereupon managed to lose the match by eight goals to nil, the Leicesters having in their ranks two players of international repute, and returned to Holt by a more recognised route, somewhat chastened.

Early in the New Year, B Company was detailed to form part of a detachment whose job it was to provide a mobile guard for the Royal Family during their stay at Sandringham, and moved to an encampment in the woods near Wolferton. As Captain Smith had become temporarily hors-de-combat as the result of having made an unprovoked attack with his Austin Seven on the wall of the bridge over the railway in Sheringham, the junior subaltern was the acting company commander. Every third day they were at five minutes' notice to move into action; the next day they were at one hour's notice; on the following day, on stand-by. Stationed nearby was a company of The Welch Regiment, whose suggestion it was that a rugger match should be played when neither they nor the RSF were on immediate notice. A local farmer, a rugby enthusiast, gave them permission to use one of his fields. This, previously grazed by cattle, was cleared and marked out with lines of creosote. Goal posts, made from a few of the many birch trees which surrounded the camp, and which were easily felled, were put in place. As most of the fusiliers were recruited from an area of Glasgow where football meant Partick Thistle or Rangers, the choice for a rugby XV was somewhat limited. The side eventually chosen after some restricted and rather chaotic practices, contained 10 volunteers with varied experience of the game, and five other reluctant 'pressed men' with none at all, to make up numbers.

All was now ready for the Scotland v Wales match. The field was close to the RSF camp, so they were considered to be the home team, and the junior subaltern arranged that suitable refreshment would be provided after play.

The Welsh XV arrived at the camp at the appointed time, and the two teams made their way through the woods to the field. On emerging from the trees, they were annoyed to find that the gate between the playing field and the adjoining meadows, into which the cows had been moved, had been left open, and the cows had returned to their previous pastures. They were even more annoyed to discover that the goalposts had vanished completely: only the gaping holes remained. The match, therefore was most definitely off. Suitable, if rather unconvincing apologies were made to the visitors, who returned to their transport and departed. There was only one other possible date for the match which suited both sides, and arrangements were made to play the game on that day.

In his role as company commander, the junior subaltern at once paid a visit to the farmer to seek a possible explanation. None was forthcoming; the farmer was as puzzled as everyone else, and extremely annoyed that the gate had been opened, and the cattle allowed to stray. He at once agreed to have the animals returned to the meadow, and to allow the field to be used for the re-arranged fixture.

Further suitable trees were felled, and new goalposts set up. A reluctant fatigue party cleared the cowpats once again, with a not-surprising lack of enthusiasm for their job. All was ready for the fixture. On the evening prior to the game, the junior subaltern checked that all was well. He was pleased to see the goal posts silhouetted tall in the moonlight, and the cows chewing the cud peacefully in the safety of the meadow. The catch on the gate was firmly secured.

On the following morning, the visitors arrived in good time; because of operational duties the kick-off time had been brought forward to 10 am; the two teams made their way to the field. It is hard to describe the feelings of the junior subaltern as he emerged at the head of the column as they left the path through the woods; for the sight before him was identical to that of the previous occasion. The meadow gate stood wide open; the cows, startled by the sudden appearance of so many rugby-clad men were off on a miniature stampede towards the further end of the field; and of goalposts there was no sign.

The stalwarts from Wales retired in some dudgeon, no doubt with very serious reservations as to the organising ability of the RSF in general, and of their B Company commander in particular, meeting as they departed the farmer coming to watch the match. As the home team helped to herd the wandering cows back to the meadow, the farmer and junior subaltern made a closer inspection of the grass. There were obvious traces to show that the goalposts had been dragged through the gateway and diagonally across the adjoining meadow to the side of a narrow path which led to the main road. At the side of the path lay small piles of sawdust. Presumably the dismantled posts had been sawn into suitable lengths and carted away.

At the end of that week, their duties at Sandringham over, B Company returned to their more normal duties at Holt. Captain Smith, having returned from hospital, was there to receive them, so the junior subaltern remained for an extra day with the rear party, to tidy up, to pay accounts, and to hear claims for compensation. In the evening, he withdrew to the local pub for what he considered to be well deserved refreshments.

It was a cold, misty evening, and the snug bar, though without any other customers, was welcoming. In the corner the flames of a generous fire threw a pleasant heat across the room. The junior subaltern carried his glass across from the bar, and sat on the highly polished bench in the inglenook, letting the sleepy warmth of the fire envelop him. The landlord, with whom earlier in the week he had struck up a slight acquaintance, drew a pint for himself and joined him on the bench.The junior subaltern commented on the excellence of the fire. The landlord agreed, saying that he liked to have a good blaze in the hearth: but it was not easy in these days. Coal was rationed, and the Sandringham estate office no longer supplied wood as it had done pre-war. No trees could be felled on Crown land, and it was forbidden to collect even fallen branches. Recently, however, he had been lucky. About a week ago, two lads were selling logs around the village for only half-a-crown a bag; by the time they had reached the pub they had only a few left, which he had taken. However, he had told them that, if ever they had more to sell, he would take the lot; moreover, he'd pay them three bob a bag. And that very evening, just before the junior subaltern had arrived, the lads had brought a whole cart-load. He had no idea where they had got the logs; these days it was best not to enquire too closely.

The landlord leant over the grate, and extracted several more logs from the large basket which stood at the side. The flames leapt higher in the chimney. The two men sat silent, gazing at the leaping flames, drinking contentedly from their pint glasses. Suddenly, one of the blazing logs fell from the banked-up fire into the hearth. The landlord, using the long pair of tongs which hung from the mantel, replaced the charred remains of the log. Where it had lain, there remained amongst the ashes in the hearth two large, shining nails. These the landlord retrieved with the tongs, remarking as he did so that such nails were hard to come by in these days of shortages: they might be useful. The nails must have been driven into the wood quite recently, being untarnished and obviously new.

Even as the landlord was in the act of replacing the burning embers, the junior subaltern's eyes had lit on these nails, for they were nails which he had immediately recognised: army issue nails, nails which could be bought in no civilian ironmonger's shop, nails of the exact type and size used by the company carpenter to affix the crossbars to the goalposts. The landlord's account of how the logs had been offered to him had already aroused his suspicions; these nails confirmed them. The mystery of the vanishing goalposts was, to him, a mystery no longer.

He gazed at the leaping flames, and considered what to do. It would be easy enough to trace the culprits who had removed the posts and converted them into these logs, whose comfort he was now enjoying; but would that really be worth all the bother that would ensue? Police involvement, court appearances, general unpleasantness. The comfort of his present surroundings brought back pleasant memories; memories of the weekly tutorial in his supervisor's rooms in Cambridge a mere 18 months ago, although it seemed far longer. He recalled the roaring fire in the room in John's New Court, the warmth, the slowly-sipped glass of pale sherry, the supervisor's comments on his essay: an essay written on the subject of Sir Robert Walpole, one of East Anglia's greatest sons.

Walpole had retained power for 21 years, his position as the first Prime Minister of England maintained by his masterly obedience to his family motto of 'Quietur Non Movere' – 'Let Sleeping Dogs Lie'.

One should always learn from history, his tutors had frequently asserted. The junior subaltern had had a difficult 10 days; why should he add to the difficulties? What was good enough for an English prime minister should surely be good enough for a junior subaltern? Let sleeping dogs lie – and army goalposts too. The decision made, he settled down in his seat, sipping occasionally at his drink, and chatting to his host.

The door of the bar opened and in came Fusilier Hickman, driver of his utility truck, bringing with him a blast of cold, damp, East Anglian air. It was time to go. Reluctant to leave his cosy corner, the junior subaltern glanced at his watch. No need to leave just yet; another 10 minutes. It was strictly against regulations to drink with other ranks, but regulations were meant to be broken from time to time. The junior subaltern ordered three pints, and Fusilier Hickman joined him and the landlord by the fireside. The three men, tankards in hand, gazed at the flames. Hickman broke the silence. "Funny thing about them goalposts, sir," he remarked, "reckon someone nicked them, sold them for logs, I reckon, made a bob or two." Suspicion again leapt to the junior subaltern's mind, as he recalled that Hickman had been one the most reluctant of the 'pressed men' for the rugger team. He glanced sideways at the fusilier, whose face showed no sign of guilt, nor indeed of any other emotion. He remembered his earlier decision, and glanced again at his watch.

"Time to go, Hickman. Drink up!" So saying, he tilted back his head to absorb the last dregs in his tankard, and got to his feet. Let sleeping dogs lie.

The two men bade farewell to the landlord and made their reluctant way out into the cold January night.

9. QUEEN BEE

For a time during the summer, the junior subaltern and 11 Platoon occupied Oak Wood, a large plantation beside the Sheringham to Weybourne road, not far from Sheringham Hall. Trenches were dug round the perimeter, and a small, revolving steel turret, designed to hold one man and a machine gun, was positioned at the junction of the main road and the track which leads across the railway to the farm near Dead Man's Hill. On sunny days this turret became unbearably hot; when rain fell, it quickly flooded. When last seen in the spring of 1949, it was encased in brambles and providing an ideal nursery for hundreds of tadpoles.

When not on immediate duty, the men lived in tents inside Oak Wood. One afternoon, soon after their arrival, the junior subaltern heard the sound of a 'plane, then the noise of gunfire. He sounded the alarm, and the men quickly took up their battle positions. A small aeroplane was crossing their front about a mile away; around it could be seen black puffs of anti-aircraft fire from the guns at Weybourne camp. The men crouched in their trenches. Only if they were directly attacked would they be given the order to fire; such were the instructions at that time under the Policy of Passive Air Defence, a policy designed to conserve precious ammunition.

At that moment the company commander rattled over the crest of the hill in his Austin Seven and drew up beside the platoon HQ situated in the widened road-side ditch. Thinking that Captain Smith was seeking shelter, the junior subaltern called on him to join them in the ditch. The company commander leant out of the car window and asked crossly, "What the hell for – what on earth are you doing?" The platoon commander, thinking perhaps that the noise of the car engine had drowned the sound of gunfire, replied, "Air raid, sir, – PAD." At the same time he pointed upwards at the 'plane, now much nearer and heading in their direction. The company commander craned his neck.

"Queen Bee, you idiot," he remarked in his usual charming fashion, revved his engine and, with the normal clashing of gears, sped off in the direction of Sheringham. The 'plane had again changed course and was heading out to sea. Firing had ceased.

The junior subaltern, completely puzzled by Captain Smith's remarks and reactions, had nevertheless learned early in his army service never to admit to ignorance. As all was now quiet, he sounded the 'All Clear', and the men returned to their camp in the centre of the wood.

That evening, off duty, he cycled into Sheringham to enjoy the comforts of the Dormy Hotel. At the bar, he met an acquaintance from Weybourne Camp, and made a casual remark about the anti-aircraft fire earlier in the day. The artillery officer was most enthusiastic in reply. The new target 'plane, the Queen Bee, radio controlled, was proving, he said, to be a great success; the brigadier had been delighted with the demonstration of target practice that afternoon. Light dawned upon the junior subaltern. "Useful to us too, you know," he said. "I made it an excuse for PAD practice. And, would you believe it, the men thought it was a real Jerry 'plane! Must arrange for them to have more aircraft recognition training when we move to Holt next month."

10. BEESTON HUMP

The junior subaltern glanced at his watch. Still 10 minutes to go until he could stand down his men at the end of a miserable hour of stand-to. It was bitterly cold there, at the top of Beeston Hump. An unpleasant mixture of rain and sleet, driven by a strong east wind, slashed across their faces as they stood peering out to sea. The muddy water in the slit trenches sloshed over their boots as they stamped their feet in a vain attempt to restore the dwindling circulation. Only the machine gunner and his mate in the pillbox had any protection from the elements, and even that was minimised, for the wind seemed to gather force as it whistled through the embrasures. The junior subaltern failed to see the purpose of these twice daily 'stand-to's'; an hour at dawn and another hour at dusk. These had no doubt been essential in the trench warfare of 1914-18, when the two opposing armies were often a mere 100 yards apart; but surely they served no useful function in the present circumstances? A vast German army could not suddenly appear on the Sheringham beaches without their approach being known for at least some hours. Indeed, the code word 'Cromwell', signifying imminent invasion, implied at least 18 hours warning. But orders were orders; and woe betide any officer who disregarded the stand-to procedures. Indeed, these times often saw visitations from members of the general staff.

He looked again at his watch. How time crept! Still another five minutes. To his left, the Sheringham sea front was now visible in the growing light, with the red pantiles made more colourful by the cleansing rain. To his right he could see the huddle of chalets on the outskirts of Cromer. The sea was rough, with the wind whipping the crests of the waves into white manes. No invasion attempt was likely in such weather. Still two minutes to go. He could feel the rain water trickling down his neck. No sign of any be-flagged car climbing the steep road which was the only direct approach to the position. It was light enough now. He blew the long blasts on his whistle to signify the stand-down. The men climbed stiffly from their slit trenches and hurried to the comparative shelter of the pillbox, leaving behind only the two unfortunates whose turn it was for outpost guard duty.

From the shelter of the entrance door to the pillbox, the junior subaltern looked across to the last house at the top of the approach road. It was a Saturday; and Saturdays and Sundays were, for a certain reason, special days for the troops on duty on Beeston Hump. The defence area encompassed the top of the hill, and had to include this one house. The house was supposedly empty, the owners living in Norwich. However, despite official regulations, the Taylor family always came to Sheringham on Friday evenings, departing on Sunday afternoons. There was a tacit agreement between the three battalion commanders whose troops occupied the position in turn, that the Taylors should be allowed to come and go. The family was most grateful (it struck the junior subaltern that it was a strange state of affairs when the owners of a property were grateful for being permitted the use of their own house). They showed their gratitude by many small acts of kindness, not the least of which was to supply the troops on duty with hot drinks after each 'stand-down' at night and in the morning. Sometimes tea, though rationing made that difficult; more often cocoa or Bovril; but always on Saturdays and Sundays each man was given this glorious, warm drink; always welcome, and a real morale-booster on a day like this.

The junior subaltern saw the back door of the house opening. The two girls came out, each carrying a couple of large jugs: from each vessel steam was rising. He licked his lips in anticipation. "Mugs ready, lads!" he called, and made his way to meet the girls who were struggling against the force of the wind, being joined on the way by his platoon sergeant and a fusilier. They met the two girls at the garden fence. Sergeant Canning and the fusilier took the jugs and returned quickly to the pillbox, to the waiting men. The junior subaltern, having warned his sergeant not to forget 'the officer's mug', chatted briefly to the girls until one fusilier returned with the empty jugs. A final word of grateful thanks from the junior subaltern, and the girls hurried back to their house, and he to the glorious steaming liquid which awaited him in the pillbox.

Every week-end for over two years the Taylors provided this kind service; even in the worst of weather, when of course the hot drink was especially appreciated, they never failed. In the house they kept a special visitors' book, into which they asked every officer who ever commanded troops on Beeston Hump to sign his name. As each battalion in the brigade changed over areas every two or three months, and each battalion moved companies and platoons about, by the end of 1942 there were very many names in the book, most with additional words of gratitude. When the junior subaltern returned to visit the area in the summer of 1949, the Taylors were still in the same house, with the visitors' book displayed proudly on the hall table, with all its names, signatures, dates, and associated memories.

On Beeston Hump there was always one section on duty, with one officer in charge, on a three-day roster. Officers had one night on duty there, one night on patrol, and the third evening free, although still on call in case of emergency. On one of his off-duty evenings, the junior subaltern was asked by his company commander to deliver a message to the officer on Beeston Hump; as usual, they were having trouble with the connecting field telephones. This suited him quite well. It was a pleasant, dry evening, and he could call in at the pub at the foot of the hill on the way back.

The message delivered, he was making his return journey down the steep street, flanked on the left by a row of terraced houses, on the right by semi-detached villas. He should reach the pub before closing time: he hoped the promised delivery of ale had materialised. His anticipatory thoughts were suddenly interrupted by the sound of a female voice calling to him from the doorway of one of the terraced houses. He stopped, for the voice sounded anxious. It was very dark; the night was moonless, and of course there was no street lighting. Many of the houses were unoccupied: the others had their windows blacked out. He could, however, make out the faint outline of a figure in the doorway. He pushed open the little gate and walked up the short path. "Please come in," said the voice. He followed the woman into a small hallway, where, having closed the door and drawn the curtains, she turned, and switched on the light.

The woman, who appeared to the junior subaltern to be of about middle age, led the way into the front lounge and invited him to be seated. She quickly revealed the reason for her fears. A few minutes ago she had opened the front door to let the cat out. Across the street, in the top window of one of the houses, she had seen a light; yet the house was supposed to be empty. She knew the owners. They had gone to live in Nottingham for the duration. The light had gone out, then reappeared at another window, faint but definite. It had then disappeared again.

Perhaps these were just reflections in the glass? The junior subaltern tried to calm her anxiety. But reflections from what? was the reply.

There was really no answer to that, for the sky was overcast, and there was no other source of light. No vehicles used that road at night. The junior subaltern felt he might be making a fool of himself; he had heard vague tales of middle-aged ladies and their fanciful stories; but this woman seemed genuinely anxious. He decided he must respond. Rather self-consciously he drew his revolver from its holster, a revolver which he had never fired in anger, and seldom even in practice.

Whilst the woman watched from her doorway, he crossed the road and went into the garden opposite. Cautiously he moved round the house, checking the front and back doors; they, and all the windows, were secured; there was no sign of any attempt at forced entry. Perhaps the owners had returned unexpectedly. He pressed the front door bell, and could hear it clearly ringing somewhere within the house. No-one came. He circled the house again, but could find nothing untoward in the masked beam of his small torch. He made his way back to the woman in the doorway, who was now holding a black cat in her arms.

They went inside, where she invited him to sit by the gas fire whilst she made some tea. The junior subaltern, realising that it was after closing time now, and that his beer would have to wait for another evening, was content to accept her offer of hospitality. She returned with a tray, tea and some biscuits. They discussed the evening, and the mysterious lights. She was adamant that she had indeed seen them. After a decent interval, the junior subaltern thanked her for the refreshment and left, telling her that if she saw the lights again, she should let him or another officer know; he gave her a number which she could telephone. It was not until he was almost back at his billet that he realised that he knew neither her name nor the name of her house. Captain Smith, his company commander, listened to his report with some scepticism. His only comment was that the woman had let her imagination run riot. She was possibly lonely and looking for male company; the junior subaltern would be advised to take a different route in future.

However, on thinking things over, the junior subaltern decided not to accept Captain Smith's advice, and at the first opportunity returned to the woman's house. She answered the bell almost immediately, and invited him in. It was still day, and she pointed out the windows in which she had seen the lights; they were easily visible from her sitting room. She had not seen the lights again. She had telephoned the owners on some pretext, not wanting to worry them, but to check they they were still in Nottingham. She had made no mention of the incident.

They chatted over a cup of tea and some biscuits. From their conversation, he learnt that she was married to a merchant sailor, who was regularly away on Atlantic convoys. She had seen him for only a few short leaves since the beginning of the war; he had little time ashore. Travel to Liverpool was not easy. Sometimes she went to meet him there, but he could never be certain when he was due into port, and hotels were expensive. The junior subaltern eventually took his leave, fully convinced that Captain Smith was wrong in his judgment and that Mrs Banks – for that was her name – was a perfectly normal, well-balanced person. The lights which she had reported were certainly not a product of her imagination.

A few days later, again on one of his evenings off duty, the junior subaltern was called to the phone by the mess corporal, to be told by an obviously excited Mrs Banks that she had seen the lights again. In fact, she could see them from her window at that very moment. It seemed, she said, as if someone was signalling, there were short and long flashes. Could he please come at once? The junior subaltern shouted to his driver and his batman, both of whom he knew would be enjoying their usual 'fly' cup of tea in the kitchen. Together they hurried to the company truck parked in the road outside. Within a matter of minutes they drew up at the foot of the road leading up the hill past Mrs Banks' house, proceeding on foot for the rest of the way. He did not want their arrival betrayed by the sound of the approaching vehicle.

Mrs Banks was at her gate when they reached her house. She pointed at a small window in the attic of the house opposite. Sure enough, they could all see a light, dim but definite, flashing intermittently. A thought crossed the junior subaltern's mind: that window faced towards the sea. Was someone signalling from the vacant house? He had some knowledge of Morse Code, and thought he could distinguish certain letters. Then the light disappeared.

His immediate inclination was to break in and arrest whomever they might find inside. On second thoughts, he decided to approach the matter with greater caution. There might be an innocent explanation. Better to have the law on one's side before damaging private property. He told the two soldiers to keep watch on the exits, and to apprehend anyone who emerged. He himself, after a quick word with Mrs Banks, hurried to the telephone to ring the local police. The law would be there as soon as possible.

He rejoined Mrs Banks at the gate. She had seen no further lights. They continued to watch until the forces of the law, represented by one elderly constable, arrived, breathless from the exertion of trying to cycle up the steep hill. The junior subaltern explained the situation. Together they watched. The constable seemed dubious, Then suddenly a light re-appeared, still faint, but on the first floor this time. As they looked, it seemed to be moving from room to room.

The junior subaltern and the constable crossed the road to join the two soldiers. A plan of action was quickly decided. The glass panel of the back door shattered easily to the blow from a soldier's rifle butt, and the four men rushed in. As planned, the two fusiliers searched the ground floor, the constable and the junior subaltern the rooms upstairs. No intruder could they find. With the aid of the policeman's lantern and a torch borrowed from Mrs Banks, they examined every conceivable hiding place. Dust covers were on the furniture, and all was as it should be. Further examination confirmed that all the windows were securely shut and bolted. There was nobody there: moreover, nobody had been there.

As puzzled as the rest of them, the policeman departed to make his report and to arrange repairs to the broken door. The junior subaltern, disappointed to have been deprived of his moment of glory – he had had fleeting visions of banner headlines, "Enemy Spy Captured by Heroic Officer' – returned to his company headquarters and a "told you so!" from Captain Smith. The account of the happenings were quick to circulate around the town (the batman had a girl friend not known for her reticence) and no doubt grew in the telling. The junior subaltern's only consolation was the knowledge that he had had the sense to insist on legal authorisation for the action, otherwise he might have been in all sorts of trouble, apart from having to pay out of his own pocket for the damage. He kept to himself the embarrassing knowledge that in the excitement of the raid he had forgotten to load the revolver which he had been brandishing so ferociously as they stormed the house, a fact which he discovered later when he came to unload the chamber and found it empty.

From time to time he dropped in to visit Mrs Banks. The lights had never returned, and they continued to puzzle over them and to discuss possible causes, without reaching any conclusion. Then, one evening, the junior subaltern called in at the Jolly Fisherman. As he stood at the bar enjoying his well-earned beer, the landlord brought up the subject, obviously interested to have some first hand news. The pub was a favourite haunt of the local fishermen, but that evening only two of the more elderly ones were there, wearing their dark blue jerseys and cloth caps, playing dominoes near the fire. Their game over, they came up to the bar. The junior subaltern, always ready to improve relationships with the civilian population – and especially the fishermen – offered drinks all round. As the landlord was drawing the ale, one of the men, obviously having overheard the conversation between the junior subaltern and the landlord, and no doubt being fully conversant with the talk that had been going around, turned to the junior subaltern and said, "reckon you'm bin a-chasing that little owd Cromer Loight, y'd nairy catch 'im, I reckon!" He then proceeded to down half the pint offered to him.

Somewhat taken aback, the junior subaltern asked for further explanation, at the same time ordering another round. The two fishermen, enjoying their unexpected free drinks, and no doubt not unaware that another might be forthcoming, continued. Most of the older people in the fishing villages, they said, had heard of the strange lights which at times would emerge from a small wood near West Runton. This had been seen by many to flit from place to place, as if in search of something, then return to its starting point and disappear. They had both seen it themselves when returning at night after fishing. Only occasionally did it alight, either on the ground or on a building. It was said by many creditable folk that a landing of the light signified that human bones were buried nearby. Someone had once dug up a place in a field where it had landed, so it was said, and found an ancient burial ground and many old coins which made his fortune. Everyone knew of the Cromer Light, as it was called. Young people didn't believe it: "Them dun know nothing!" Foreigners (an East Anglian term for anyone who is not a native) had various explanations for this phenomenon. Some said that it was the reflection of the beam of the Cromer lighthouse on banks of fog: but the phenomenon could appear on a clear night. Others suggested it was similar to the Will o' the Wisp; but that was known to be caused by gases from an area of bog-land, and the land here was dry and sandy. Indeed, the junior subaltern had, when very small, often seen the Will o' the Wisp dancing over the peat bogs from which the distillery near his home obtained its special water; that was quite different.

Gratified by the attention given to their joint explanations, and even more so by the offer of another pint, the fishermen gave it as their considered opinion that it must indeed have been the Cromer Light which the junior subaltern had seen. They even went so far as to suggest he might try digging up the garden of that house to expose the human bones which would undoubtedly be there!

The junior subaltern did not, of course, pass on this explanation to his company commander; he knew all too well how that would be received. The incident was soon forgotten, except by the principal participants. He occasionally called in to see Mrs Banks on his way to and from the Hump, and they talked the matter over from time to time, without getting any nearer to any logical conclusion. She had informed the house owners that their back door had been broken and subsequently repaired, without giving the true cause of the damage. Towards the end of the year she moved to a rented house in Liverpool, where she and her husband, on leave at the time, were both unfortunately killed in an air raid: thus the junior subaltern learnt by chance some months later, when the battalion had moved elsewhere.

The remains of the pillbox still stand on Beeston Hump, close now to the clifftop because of the erosion of 50 years. New houses have sprung up around, but not on the Hump. The Taylors' home is still much as it was in those days. Mrs Banks' former house seems to have changed outwardly not at all. Much, though, is altered across the road, where additions have been built. Were any human bones discovered during the alterations? The junior subaltern would like to know; but there are some hidden things that are best kept secret. The Cromer Light must be one of these.

11. BEN OF HOLT

Everybody knew him as Ben. Presumably he had a surname, but the junior subaltern had never heard it, nor had met anyone else who used it. Ben owned an ancient, beautiful black Rolls Royce hearse which, with minimum and almost instant modification could be, as required, converted into a taxi, a wedding car, a trademan's van or what nowadays would be called a mini-bus. In a time of petrol shortage and rationing, Ben and his Rolls never seemed to go short of this essential; in his own words, he had 'sources'. Ben himself was as versatile as his vehicle ('car' is too insignificant a word to use in this instance). Undertaker, taxi driver, 'bus driver, carpenter, glazier; even chimney sweep, for one day the junior subaltern, passing unsteadily at the head of his flying bicycle picket, saw the Rolls parked outside Holt rectory, with the brushes and other accoutrements of a sweep plainly visible through the glass panels.

Ben was always suitably dressed for the occasion. At a funeral he would be in morning coat, a little shabby perhaps, but neatly pressed, with well brushed shining top hat; the silver and chrome on the Rolls would be draped decorously in mourning crêpe. For weddings, the bride would drive to church in a gaily bedecked Rolls, Ben at the wheel dressed in a smart blue suit and chauffeur's cap. When the Rolls served as a mini-bus, Ben adopted a more relaxed fashion, but was still smart in grey flannels and nautical blue blazer. He was of indeterminate age, and seemed to change, chameleon-like, to blend with his surroundings and with the occasion. Ben was in great demand, not only with the local inhabitants of Holt and district, but also with the officers of The Royal Scots Fusiliers whose mess was in the sanitorium of Gresham's School. There were few opportunities for relaxation in those days when invasion seemed imminent: yet relaxation was essential for young men under strain, when morale had to be kept high. Whichever battalion was currently based at Gresham's School was always the reserve for the brigade, and so had greater opportunity to enjoy precious time off than had the forward battalions on the coast.

Perhaps once or twice in a month the assistant adjutant arranged an evening in Norwich for those officers who were interested, and off duty at the time, perhaps five or six. These numbers were increased to a maximum of twelve by individual officers of the nearby units, with perhaps the odd WAAF or ATS who wanted a lift to Norwich. This was the most which could be accommodated in the Rolls; for it was to Ben, in his office tucked away behind The Feathers (in the area where Budgens now stands) that they turned for transport. Army vehicles could not be used for such recreational purposes.

Ben always seemed delighted to make himself and his Rolls available on such occasions. A bench was fixed down each side of the vehicle, and a coffin from his workshop placed down the centre to give greater stability. Thus twelve passengers could be seated somewhat uncomfortably. The charge for the evening was very reasonable, and divided equally. The officers of the RSF, being the bulk of the party, paid Ben in advance. Individual officers, picked up *en route*, were expected to pay their share at the start of their journey. On arrival at Norwich, the officers always had a ‘whip-round’ to collect a good tip for Ben. It was a most satisfactory arrangement for all concerned.

During the battalion’s first spell in Holt, these occasional trips to Norwich went very well. The officers kept to a similar pattern each time. Ben parked the Rolls near the centre of the city and, a departure time having been agreed, the officers and Ben went their respective ways. Usually, the RSF group kept together, visiting first The Castle and The Bell, before finishing the evening at The Sampson and Hercules, where many of the others on the dance floor felt that the tartan trews gave the RSF an unfair advantage. Nobody knew how Ben spent his time. He said he visited ‘contacts’; most of these seemed to inhabit or frequent various hostelries in Tombland, and the junior subaltern suspected that much of his ‘gratuity’ was expended there. Sometimes the Rolls’ progress on the return journey was more erratic than on the outward one; but the roads were deserted of traffic, the breathalyser was a thing of the future, and nobody worried much. Indeed, it was generally agreed that the Rolls could probably find its own way back to Holt. The usual convivial songs were sung. Ben would sometimes contribute some unintelligible Norfolk ditty in a throaty tenor; and hearty “goodnights” were given to those dropped off at intermediate destinations.

A difficulty, however, arose during the battalion's second period in Holt. The outgoing Leicesters, whom the RSF had replaced in Gresham's School, had warned the assistant adjutant that the Norwich trips, which they had maintained, were being spoilt by the attitude and behaviour of a certain Royal Artillery officer, a captain on an anti-aircraft site a few miles out of Holt. This officer had tried to use his higher rank to interfere with the arrangements; he had also shown a certain reluctance to pay his share of what was the extremely reasonable charge made for the evening's journey. He had also upset Ben, who was threatening to withdraw his services. The RSF assistant adjutant noted these accusations but, not wanting to cause friction with a neighbouring unit, decided to let things be for the present, and to see what happened.

On their first outing, the Rolls stopped near the AA site to pick up the RA captain. The gunner caused immediate offence by insisting that as he outranked everyone present, he was entitled to the best seat in the front, beside Ben. He thereupon ordered the RSF officer seated there to move to the back, while he took the vacated seat. On arrival at Norwich the captain declined to contribute the customary tip for Ben; he said he disapproved of such a practice. He then disagreed with the time chosen to begin the return journey. The RSF officers were not impressed, and on their return reported their displeasure to the assistant adjutant.

Together the latter and Ben concocted a plan which they hoped would deal with the situation, and which would avoid the necessity of making a formal complaint. Ben was only too pleased to become involved: his opinion of the RA officer had already been expressed in no uncertain terms, whilst he had always enjoyed the company of the others. Before the next trip, the two of them had several meetings in Ben's little office, and later were to be seen in the bar of The Feathers conferring with Steevie, an officer in A Company. Steevie was reputed to be the smallest officer in the British Army.

"Five feet no inches in army boots," he would proudly assert: "Good gear in little bulk." Despite his lack of inches, he was extremely strong. Rumour – via his batman – had it that he indulged privately in body-building exercises. Steevie reckoned he was bound to survive the war; the Germans would always be firing too high to hit him! He was also an inveterate practical joker, a trait which had frequently led him into trouble with authority.

When the RSF officers assembled for the next Norwich trip, they were surprised to find that Major North had joined the party, for normally the evening was restricted to junior officers. When the Rolls drew up at the mess, Jocky North took the passenger seat; the others clambered into the back, taking their places on the usual benches and on the coffin in the centre. When they stopped to pick up the RA officer, they realised the reason for the inclusion of the major in their party. The gunner captain marched briskly to the front of the Rolls, opened the passenger door and said, "My seat, I think!" Then, as the occupant did not move, nor reply, he looked up to see the field officer's crown insignia on Jocky North's shoulder. It was a crestfallen gunner who, muttering some apology, closed the door and moved to the rear of the vehicle to take a precarious and less comfortable seat on the end of the central coffin.

Once in Norwich and Ben's collection made, again without contribution from the gunner officer, the RSF party headed for The Bell. There, Jocky North ordered a round of drinks and gathered the others around him in a corner of the lounge bar. The young officers listened with approval to the plan which he disclosed to them, one intended to discourage the unpleasant RA officer from ever joining them again. They were given their instructions, the final one being to assemble at the Rolls at least 15 minutes before the arranged time of departure. The major then went off with Steevie, leaving the others to enjoy the evening in their customary fashion.

As instructed, the RSF officers returned to Castle Hill and the parked Rolls to find Jocky North, Steevie and Ben already there. The coffin 'seat' in the centre of the vehicle had its lid raised, and Steevie was in the act of climbing in. As he lay down in the coffin, Ben passed him a cushion to place beneath his head, and then gently lowered the lid, whilst the major inserted two small wooden wedges, so that a gap was left between lid and box which would admit sufficient air. Steevie's muffled voice assured them that he was all right. The other officers took their places as previously agreed, leaving room for the RA captain – the only 'outsider' on this occasion – on the near-side bench, facing the hinged side of the coffin.

The captain came at the agreed time, surprised to find that he was the last to arrive. Normally people tended to drift up late, a cause of some complaint from the RA officer. Soon the Rolls was off on its return journey. Ben had opened the glass partition which separated the front seats from the hearse part of the vehicle. He often did this, as he liked both to take part in the general sing-song, and also to make his own individual Norfolk contributions. The officers were, to the RA officer's relief, somewhat more subdued than usual; the latter did not approve of their normal ‘childish’ behaviour. The songs died out completely. With the glass partition open, any conversation between Jocky North and Ben could now easily be overheard by those in the back. As they approached Corpusty, Ben’s voice could be heard very clearly. The junior subaltern could not help but notice that the gunner captain, seated in an advantageous position, was listening closely to every word. They could all, indeed, follow the conversation.

It appeared that Ben had an important funeral in the morning. This, he explained to Major North, was to be held much earlier in the day than usual, as some VIPs were attending who had to return to London quickly for an important meeting. To save time, Ben went on, he had made some advance preparations that afternoon, before they left for Norwich. Jocky North expressed interest, asking the nature of these preparations. Ben, adopting a conspiratorial tone, replied in a sort of stage whisper: the corpse, he told the major, was already laid out in the coffin behind them, the one which was being used as a seat. The body would come to no harm, and he hadn’t mentioned it the passengers, so nobody was any the worse for his pre-funeral arrangements. It would save a great deal of time in the morning. The RSF officers were talking quietly amongst themselves, studiously pretending not to have overheard the conversation in the front. The gunner captain, all ears, had obviously assimilated every word which passed between Ben and the major: the junior subaltern, glancing to his left, thought that he had gone pale. In the dim light he could see him staring with apprehension and distaste at the coffin in front of him.

At a pre-arranged but hidden signal, the singing which had begun again, stopped abruptly. In the sudden silence, an eerie, scraping sound could be heard coming from the coffin. This was followed by a loud moan. The coffin lid began to rise, very slowly. Those sitting on it, forewarned, rose gently with it. Another groan (don’t overdo it, Steevie, the junior subaltern said to himself). Further scratching sounds. A damp, musty, earthy odour, apparently emanating from the coffin, permeated the Rolls. More scratching sounds. The air suddenly seemed chill, even to those in the know. Then over the edge of the box, in the gap left by the rising lid, appeared the outline of a human hand, the knuckles glowing in the darkness.

There was another sudden sound, that of the RA officer being noisily sick. Ben braked, and the Rolls drew up at the side of the road. Someone opened the rear door, and the RA officer scrambled out. “Your site is just up the hill there,” said Jocky North pointing into the darkness with

Then over the edge... in the gap left by the rising lid, appeared the outline of a human hand, the knuckles glowing in the darkness.

his cane, "only a couple of minutes' walk. Goodnight, hope you're better in the morning!" The Rolls moved off again, one passenger short; a passenger faced with a somewhat lengthy walk, for the major's estimate of the distance to the anti-aircraft site had been by no means accurate. A few minutes later, on the outskirts of Holt, Ben stopped the Rolls once more to allow Steevie out of his rather cramped and uncomfortable resting place. He emerged, stiff but triumphant, to the laughter and applause of his fellow passengers, holding in one hand one of these 'party-props' which could be obtained in any of the little trick shops to be found in most towns, and which were widely advertised in children's comics: the skeleton of a human hand with the bones outlined in luminous paint. He leant into the coffin, and lifted out a small khaki satchel, whence the unpleasant smell had come. This he passed to the officer nearest the door, who hurriedly emptied on to the verge of the road its mixed contents of damp earth and decaying leaves. The coffin lid closed, and seats resumed, the Rolls completed the journey.

As they passed through the sleeping town the 'ghostly' hand was passed along the row for closer inspection amid much laughter, until the officer at the back, who had been leaning out and waving the hand in the hopes that it might become a thing of wonder to any Holt insomniac who might be watching, let it drop. For a few brief moments the hand could be seen glowing in the gutter, till the Rolls swung round the bend at the end of the street and it was gone from sight. The junior subaltern hoped it might be picked up the following morning by some schoolboy, to become a treasured possession in the local school.

When they climbed down from the Rolls at the gates of the officers' mess he remarked to Ben that he hoped he would not be too tired for the funeral in the morning. "What funeral?" exclaimed Ben, "who mentioned a funeral?" His face was a picture of innocence as he stood in the shaded beam of the headlights. "I'm off fishing near Yarmouth, first thing!"

It was a month before another trip to Norwich could be arranged. In the interim, a message was received from the RA battery at Edgefield Green, to say that unfortunately, because of increased operational duties, their captain would no longer be able to come on these expeditions in future. They would therefore be obliged if his name could be removed from the list.

It was with no little satisfaction that the assistant adjutant dipped his pen deep into his bottle of red ink, used for all cancellations, and complied with this request.

12. FRONT LINE HOTELS

By the autumn of 1940, few of the hotels on the north Norfolk coast were open for normal business. Visitors were not allowed into the area, so there was little demand for accommodation. Bar trade was limited by the difficulties of obtaining supplies, and those pubs and bars which remained open tended to serve regular customers only. In the coastal towns and villages between East Runton and Blakeney, the only hotels known to the junior subaltern which still provided accommodation were the Manor Hotel in Blakeney and the Dormy (now called 'The Highwayman') in Sheringham. Most of the larger hotels had been taken over by the army for the billeting of soldiers, or to serve as headquarters or offices.

In Sheringham, the Grand and the Burlington on the promenade, as well as the Sheringham Hotel at the junction of the main coast road and the Holt road, were all commandeered. The small Rose Hotel in East Runton was a company officers' mess. The Blakeney Hotel on the quayside at Blakeney was in similar use. Further to the west, the Victoria Hotel at Holkham was still in operation, but all the bedrooms were permanently occupied by army officers, for whom the dining room was also reserved, and soldiers were billeted in the annexe. As a reminder of this fact, and a gesture of gratitude to the manageress, Mrs Smith, it was arranged for the regimental artist to engrave on the glass panels of the door which led into the bar from the lounge the insignia of each of the regiments whose officers were at one time or another staying at the Victoria.

At that stage in the war, the Army Quartermaster's Department was still very peace-time orientated in its attitude and organisation. Everything used had to be accounted for, usually in triplicate. Any loss had to be justified before any replacement was made. This applied even to ammunition. There was little opportunity for rifle or revolver practice, because of shortages, but if any took place, then the requisition (in triplicate) for replacement ammunition had to be accompanied by the exact number of used cartridge cases. The junior subaltern often wondered what would happen when the enemy attacked and he and his men had used up their few rounds of ammunition. Would the QM's Department at last relax its precious rules? He had nightmares in which he saw his men scurrying around picking up all their used cartridge cases, whilst the Germans walked ashore unopposed.

The same rigid rules applied to requisitioned buildings. When one unit handed over to another a complete list of damages and deficiencies had to be agreed. Any discrepancy was the fault and the responsibility of the outgoing unit, and was chargeable to that unit. This of course led to all sorts of practices and deceptions being attempted by the officer handing over: likewise the officer of the incoming unit would be aware of his opposite number's intentions, and do his best to combat them.

It fell to the lot of the junior subaltern to have to take over the Grand Hotel in Sheringham. He stood in the large, empty entrance hall, gazing around him, waiting for the arrival of the officer from whom he was to accept the building. His company commander's dire warnings were still, in his ears, "Check everything and then check again, or else you'll be done: I know that lot, they'd cheat their own grandmothers!"

Being completely new to this kind of transaction, he had brought his platoon sergeant, Bert Canning, along with him: a regular soldier, well versed and experienced in the wiles of army life. Their opposite number, a regular quartermaster who had been commissioned from the ranks, needed no such support. Sergeant Canning knew him of old, and warned his platoon commander. "Don't sign anything, sir, until I've checked," were his final words as the other officer entered the hall through the open front doors.

The Grand was a large hotel, and in its emptiness seemed vast. Each room was checked: windows, cupboards, light bulbs, the lot. Discrepancies and breakages were noted on the requisition sheets. A hurried 'haversack lunch', and on they went, till the attics were reached and checked. Finally, downstairs again, and to the various outbuildings; all was complete, and both sides satisfied. The officers each signed the sheets, each kept a copy, with a third sent to Brigade.

It had been a tiring day, and the junior subaltern was glad he had decided that his sergeant and himself should stay at the Grand overnight. The next day they would have time in the morning to learn more about the building, and to allocate the rooms for their various purposes. Each selected a room for the night, dumped their bedding equipment, and went out in search of the nearest open café for an evening meal. On their return the Grand was in complete darkness, the electricity having been cut off prior to a meter reading being taken on completion of the handover. Both, knowing this, had brought their torches. It was strange to be in such a large, empty building: at least 70 rooms, and just the two of them. Their feet echoed on the bare steps as they climbed to the second floor, where each had selected a room which overlooked the sea.

The junior subaltern was in the process of unrolling his sleeping bag on the uncarpeted floorboards when he heard the sound of his sergeant's footsteps clumping along the passage. A knock at the door, and Sergeant Canning came in. "He's done us, sir," he exclaimed angrily, "he's done us, the wily old b----! Come and have a look!" The junior subaltern re-laced his boots and followed his sergeant up to the attic. Canning moved over to where a stack of old bedsteads had been piled against one wall, several of which he had pulled to one side to reveal a door, one which they had not previously noticed. The sergeant opened this and shone his torch through the opening, to disclose a large bathroom, complete with bath, several washbasins, mirrors, and a shower. In the far corner were two WC cubicles.

This area had presumably been part of the hotel staff quarters. The officer followed his sergeant in. To his dismay, the light of their torches disclosed several cracked mirrors, plugs missing from the bath and basins, a broken window, minor damage to WCs and basins. Being unaware of the very existence of this bathroom, he, of course, had signed the requisition forms without registering any of these deficiencies and imperfections. The two men, their inspection completed, retraced their steps, the sergeant replacing the old bedsteads across the door.

On his hard and uncomfortable bedroll, the junior subaltern lay awake and wondered what he could do. If his company commander heard of this, he would be furious. He could, of course, say nothing, and hope that, when he in his turn came to hand over the building to the in-coming battalion, he could in the same way conceal and pass on the liabilities which he had unwittingly inherited. However, it was quite possible that he would be handing over to the same battalion and to the same quartermaster, whose triumph would then be complete, as would be his own downfall. What would then happen to him, the junior subaltern? Official reprimand? Pay deductions for damages? Certainly the wrath of his company commander. Perhaps Sergeant Canning would produce some solution in the morning. Troubled by these thoughts, he eventually fell asleep.

He was awoken by the sound of a loud explosion, and the noise of shattering glass, some of which had splintered over the floor and on to the bed. Then a series of minor explosions, with further tinkling glass. Struggling into his cold boots, he crunched to the gaping hole which had been the window of his room; looking out he narrowly escaped decapitation from a landslide of falling roof tiles. Smoke was rising from the nearby shingle; obviously the large primary explosion had caused sympathetic detonation of the mines laid on the shore, the smell of explosive filled his nostrils. He could hear the fading drone of a departing aircraft.

The sound of Sergeant Canning clattering down the stairs made him turn back into the room. His initial words were stifled by the sergeant's, "Good old Jerry, come and see, sir!" Once again he followed the sergeant aloft, taking the stairs two at a time, till they reached the attic. The stack of old bedsteads was illuminated by the light of a full moon, for there were now great gaps in the ceiling and in the roof above. The sergeant pulled back the bedsteads and opened the door to the bathroom. This had lost even more of its ceiling, and nearly all the roof tiles had disappeared. Bath and basins were filled with debris; one mirror lay smashed on the floor, another hung, cracked and chipped from a remaining hook. It must have been only a small bomb which the enemy 'plane had dropped, but one powerful enough to cover all the deficiencies and discrepancies which the junior subaltern had failed to record. It did not need Sergeant Canning to remind him that there was one excuse that even the Quartermaster's Department could not refuse to recognise as a justifiable reason for damage or loss: 'destroyed by enemy action'.

Together the junior subaltern and his sergeant returned down the stairs and to their respective rooms. There would be much clearing up and re-checking to be done in the morning, but that was of little matter. His worries over the attic bathroom were no more. He could keep to himself the knowledge that he had been outsmarted by the other regiment's QM; there would be no need to suffer the rage of Captain Smith; he might even receive some complimentary remarks, though that was perhaps expecting a bit too much. He brushed away some clinging splinters of glass, and snuggled down into his sleeping bag, to enjoy the remainder of the night in untroubled and unworried slumber.

13. EXERCISES AND MANOEUVRES

During 1940, from the time of Dunkirk onwards, and throughout 1941, not much time was devoted to training exercises on anything but a small and local scale. Because of the immediate threat of invasion, it was obviously inadvisable for the troops on coastal defences to move any great distance from their defence positions. These themselves were still incomplete, and the soldiers spent most of their time working to improve them. Indeed, it was well into 1942 before the building of pillboxes and gun emplacements was finished.

Early training exercises were therefore based on individual sections and platoons, with the need to practice the actual defence of their own particular sectors. These schemes would last for an hour or so at the most. The battalion in reserve at Holt might embark on slightly more ambitious manoeuvres lasting for a whole day or night.

As the threat of imminent invasion receded, it was thought possible to attempt slightly wider schemes, involving the whole brigade, with adequate precautions taken against a sudden enemy raid. These exercises were all based on improving defence tactics, and the 'story' was always much the same, although locations and incidents could vary. The 'enemy' would have landed somewhere in the brigade sector, and would be represented by one of the forward battalions, whose objective would be Norwich or Swaffham or Bury St. Edmunds. The defenders would be the reserve battalion stationed in Holt, whose task it was to deny the enemy until the divisional reserves held around Cambridge could be brought forward. That was the usual exercise 'story'. At times the Home Guard might be given a part to play.

These exercises were, by their very nature, extremely artificial. They had to develop according to a previously decided pattern involving time and areas. A 12-hour scheme had to last for 12 hours, not for 16 nor for three. Built-up areas and farm land had to be avoided. Civilian traffic could not be disrupted. It would never do, for instance, for the ‘defender’ to be completely over-run in the first few hours of a 24-hour exercise. Similarly, an attack could not be made using private gardens as an approach even though that approach was technically the most suitable.

Umpires were appointed to ensure that these and other details were taken care of; they alone knew the ‘rules’ of the particular scheme, and it was their task, and no easy one, to see that all ran according to plan. Their task was made all the more difficult because they were usually of lesser rank than those whom they had to control. They were also few in number. Ambitious officers, eager to display their capabilities, were not averse to taking advantage of any umpiring error or omission. To be appointed an umpire on exercises or manoeuvres was therefore not something to be desired. The junior subaltern always tried to avoid such a duty, but with only limited success.

Exercises which involved members of the LDV or Home Guard could make life especially difficult for a junior umpire, for several and various reasons. Home Guard platoons tended to contain some retired First World War officers of high rank who were most dismissive of any artificial obstacles which might be placed in their way by an umpire. If told that he could not advance up a road because an ‘imaginary’ tank blocked his way, the Home Guard commander was likely to reply that he couldn’t see any tank, and continue on his planned attack. He wasn’t going to be dictated to by a mere pip-squeak of a second-lieutenant, umpire arm-band or no, who insisted on seeing a tank where none existed. (This need to ‘imagine’ vehicles and weapons, although essential because of the shortage then of the real thing, put an additional burden on the poor umpires).

Because of their civilian duties, and to avoid disrupting these, Home Guard involvement was usually restricted to evenings or week-ends, which did not always please those members of the Home Guard, very young or perhaps retired, whose time was free. Occasionally an umpire would find his carefully prepared scenario wrecked by the sudden unscripted intervention of an HG section, or by individual Home Guards using their initiative. One umpire once waited in vain for the planned arrival of a company’s ‘O’ Group at a crossroads near Aylmerton Row. On investigating the reason for the group’s non-appearance, he found the furious officers locked in a nearby barn. guarded by a few proud members of the local Home Guard, who had voluntarily joined ‘the battle’. The wretched umpire had not only to resolve the problem without causing undue offence, but also to placate the irate farmer on whose premises this unexpected action had taken place. In the meantime, of course, the whole timing of the exercise had been disrupted.

Farmland, especially growing crops, was sacrosanct. This, in the part of East Anglia in which the junior subaltern and his brigade were stationed, made it hard to find a suitable area for manoeuvres. And so, much more make-believe and artificiality was required than, for instance, in the Breckland region; thus the difficulties of umpires were compounded.

The junior subaltern was acting as one of the umpires in a small exercise designed to test the defences at Pretty Corner, behind Sheringham, during the early summer of 1941. A thick copse near the top of the hill, beside the crossroads, was occupied by the defenders. The obvious approach for the attack was through the standing corn in a field bordering the copse; but of course this route could not be allowed, except in theory, to avoid damaging crops. So he, as the umpire on the spot, had to explain to the officer commanding the defence that they could not fire on the 'enemy' marching openly up the road towards them, as the 'enemy' troop were really concealed in the standing corn. A few minutes later he was trying to explain to a disgruntled attacking platoon commander that his men couldn't fire on the defenders whom they could see withdrawing from the copse. "Why not?" "Because you are really in the corn field, and can't see them or bring fire to bear!"

An extra complication for the umpires was the need to allow for imaginary or substitute weapons and vehicles. Even as late as the summer of 1941 there were few units which were up to establishment in firepower or transport. One Bren gun carrier might have to represent a squadron of tanks; a rifle might be labelled an anti-tank gun. Any such representation had to be explained by the umpires to the 'combatants', who were seldom willing to acknowledge such fictions when they interfered with their tactical plans. All in all, it might well be said that an umpire's lot was not a happy one.

Only once, however, in his admittedly few umpiring experiences, did the junior subaltern find himself in serious difficulties. This was on one of the bigger exercises, held in the Breckland area, where there were greater opportunities for open and mechanised movement than on the coast. His own battalion was not involved, being at that time temporarily detached in Swaffham, engaged often on fire-fighting duties extinguishing the many heath fires of that hot summer. He for once disobeyed the army axiom of never volunteering for anything; he disliked the umpire's duties, but disliked even more the hot, thirsty, dusty work the battalion was engaged upon, and added his name to the umpiring detail.

According to the scenario given to the umpires for this exercise, the 'Red' army had landed in strength by sea, reinforced by parachute troops dropped around Thetford. The invaders were advancing on Cambridge. It was a two-day scheme; during the first day the defenders were to conduct a fighting withdrawal, and by evening were to be holding a line on the far bank of the River Lark between Mildenhall and Fornham St. Martin. The second day was to begin with an attempt by the Red army to establish a bridgehead over the river; the 'White' army (the defenders) were to prevent either the establishment of such bridgeheads, or to contain them. The umpires at their briefing were given detailed instructions about boundaries, times, local difficulties, and so on, about which of course the participating Red and White armies were in ignorance. It was explained to the umpires – though of course unknown to the combatants – that the Red army should be brought to a halt at the end of the first day along the near bank of the river, and not be allowed to cross it; the scenario for the second day must open with the planned crossing – or defence – of the river.

Each umpire had his own assignment, with a senior umpire in overall control. The junior subaltern's duties were light on the first day, but he had a vital role in the evening to ensure that the Red army's leading troops did not cross the bridge over the River Lark at Barton Mills. He had firm orders to instruct their leading column that the bridge had been blown, and that the crossing was covered by machine gun fire from two pillboxes manned by a platoon of local Home Guards. (These defenders would be imaginary at that time, but at dawn the following morning, Saturday, the Home Guard would be in and around the pillboxes in person). This bridge would be a central point in the action on the second day of the exercise; it must not be crossed on the first day.

According to the umpire's time schedule, the earliest that the leading elements of the Red army could reach the bridge was 1830 hours. The junior subaltern, having witnessed a minor skirmish around the crossroads at Elvedon, set out on his bicycle on the six miles to Barton Mills in good time. Then disaster! Punctures in both tyres. Leaving his useless cycle at the side of the road, he continued on foot, hoping against hope that he would reach the bridge before the leading sections of the Red army arrived. Panting, out of breath, he arrived at the road junction near the river, only to see, to his utter dismay, troops of the attacking army moving along the opposite bank and heading up the slope towards the two pillboxes. On the 'blown' bridge itself stood a Bren gun carrier, from which an officer was watching through binoculars the progress of the troops.

The wretched umpire was appalled. With a bridgehead across the Lark already established by the Red army, the whole time table of the exercise would be thrown out of gear. The exercise itself would be wrecked; and his would be the blame. He approached the carrier on the bridge. The officer was known to him; a major whom he had met briefly whilst on a course at Sandy. He saluted smartly, telling the major that the bridge was blown, that the pillboxes were manned by machine guns, and that unless he withdrew his men and himself to the near bank, the major and his men would be considered casualties by the umpires. The junior subaltern was taking a big risk in this, for it was not in his script to determine casualties in this way; but he felt the bluff was his only chance.

Greatly superior to him in rank, the major looked at the umpire, then spoke quietly but determinedly, "This bridge has not been blown, and my men report that the pillboxes are not manned; and if you are stupid enough to make us casualties, you'll wreck the whole exercise – so on we go!"

His bluff called, the junior subaltern made one more effort to avoid disaster. He explained exactly what had happened, and appealed to the major's good nature. The major's good nature was not much in evidence; he had captured the bridge, and had used his initiative to good effect in the battle. No umpire had been there to deny him. What he had, he was going to hold. He wasn't going to withdraw just to oblige a young second-lieutenant who had been foolish enough to arrive late on the scene.

The unhappy umpire decided to try to bargain. If the major would withdraw, then he, the umpire, would disclose all his instructions for the following day, with all the dispositions and plans of the White army set out in detail. The major could then, knowing all about the enemy, have a field day. Moreover, on this side of the river there was a convenient pub, still well stocked, which he could use as a comfortable HQ for the night. The major, recognising a good thing when he saw one, withdrew his men and his carrier. The umpire thankfully placed in position his 'Bridge Destroyed' sign. He, and the exercise, had been saved.

At the 'post-mortem' held in Cambridge a few days later to discuss the course of the exercise, and to note the lessons learnt, the brigadier made special mention of Major Philips of the Red army. This officer, said the brigadier, had shown a very intelligent appreciation of the situation on the second day, had displayed great determination and initiative, and was to be specially commended on the skill shown in the river crossing. The junior subaltern glanced to his left to where the major was sitting, to be answered by a conspiratorial wink. The umpires were thanked for their contribution to what was considered to have been a successful exercise. One of their number, greatly relieved at the final outcome, was more than happy to surrender his arm-band and to return to his battalion in Swaffham. The prospect of fighting heath fires in mid-summer did not seem quite so unpleasant after all.

14. ALL ROUND DEFENCE

Even today, over 50 years on, there remain many traces of the junior subaltern's fusiliers along the north Norfolk coast. There are the obvious reminders of their stay, those constructed of more durable materials: pillboxes, gun positions, anti-tank obstacles, iron scaffolding. Time, tide, erosion, weather and human destruction have all taken their toll; but some, such as the main pillbox on Weybourne Hope, have survived remarkably well. Some, a little further inland, have been converted for peaceful uses: the sword turned to ploughshare. Other traces are less recognisable, more difficult to find unless one knows, or remembers, their exact locations. These are the remnants of the slit trenches, the dug-outs and the underground shelters which he and his men excavated. Together they dug holes at East Runton gap and on the side of Stone Hill overlooking the railway line as it swings in a great curve towards Cromer station. They helped civilian contractors to build the pillbox on Beeston Hump, of which nothing now remains save a small circle of cement. The small hollow on the very edge of the cliff is all that is left of a pit in which grenades were stored. Further erosion will soon sweep even that away.

Sheringham golfers will no doubt have encountered valleys which did not exist on the course pre-war. Walkers on the heathland around Pretty Corner near the Upper Sheringham crossroads may stumble upon, or into, unexpected holes amongst the heather. There is a small bridge which carries a farm track from the main road across the railway line and towards the sea at Dead Man's Hill, between Sheringham and Weybourne. In the bank, on both sides of the bridge, and close to the farm buildings which in 1941 served as B Company HQ, there are hollows which 50 years ago held the section posts dug to cover the railway cutting. On cold winter days, the locomotive drivers of the old Midland and Great Northern Railway trains sometimes stopped for a quick moment to supply the soldiers on duty with cans of boiling water for a ‘brew up’. (The railway was unkindly and widely known as the Muddle and Go Nowhere.) The remains of a secondary pillbox on Weybourne Hope now sit drunkenly on the shingle, in company with some resilient anti-tank blocks. The list is never-ending. There were over 40 pillboxes, to say nothing of the other defence works erected or excavated or converted during the two years beginning in the early summer of 1940, all along the narrow coastal strip between Cromer and Holkham, with which the junior subaltern and his men were to a greater or lesser extent acquainted. Those mentioned are but a few examples of what remains of the coastal defences of those days, as much a part of British history as the Martello towers of an earlier invasion threat in Napoleonic times.

Some of the earliest constructions, built in the days of great urgency and anxiety immediately after Dunkirk, were later found to be of little use. They had to be altered or re-positioned. Several pillboxes taken over by 11 Platoon had obviously been erected without due consideration being given to the local farmer’s intentions. A magnificent field of corn had since grown up; observation had become completely obscured. Fortunately, a fine summer meant an early harvest, and the restoration of the field of fire from the pillboxes concerned. Urgent consultation with the farmer ensured that such a situation did not arise the following summer.

One of the most useless and the most curious defence constructions which came under the temporary command of the junior subaltern was the revolving steel turret, mentioned in Chapter 9, which was sited at a track-road junction beside Oak Wood, between Weybourne and Sheringham. Intended to hold one man, it must have been designed by someone with sadistic inclinations. The turret in summer became at times unbearably hot; in winter, diabolically cold. In wet weather, it took in water easily. It had a good field of fire, assuming that the unfortunate occupant could manage both to manipulate the turning mechanism and also find the room within its confines to bring his gun to bear, and to change the Bren magazines. The commander of 11 Platoon chose to find alternative accommodation for his machine gunner, as did most of the other platoon commanders when their turn came to man Oak Wood. The turret, rusting up, soon ceased to revolve. It is now no longer there: perhaps someone has at last found some suitable use for it.

The junior subaltern’s first battle position in the front line was a slightly unusual one. For about a fortnight after the battalion had moved from Melton Mowbray, and previous to their occupation of the north Norfolk coastline, the 11th RSF were stationed temporarily in Great Yarmouth and in Caister holiday camp. He, with his 11 Platoon, was given a three-storey building on the town front, near Wellington Pier. This they had to convert into a military strong-point; it was also their living quarters.

Two rooms on the first floor, giving good all round observation, with a field of fire covering the street and the beach, were selected to form the strong-point. The building seemed altogether too flimsy for its intended purpose, but his job was not to question why. The first few hours were spent in filling sandbags and reinforcing with them the walls and windows of the two rooms, in one of which the floor, unused to the weight of so much sand, suddenly developed an alarming list. The situation was more or less restored with the help of some floorboards removed from the attics. By the first evening, the junior subaltern was able to survey the coastal scene from his sandbagged window with some satisfaction. Outwardly, it looked quite good. How his defence post would survive any sort of enemy onslaught was a matter upon which he preferred not to dwell.

The members of 11 Platoon found this Yarmouth post greatly to their liking. The men were recruited mainly from the humbler environments of Glasgow, and what they might lack in military efficiency they more than made up for in natural cunning. They were experts in the army art of 'winning' things, of scrounging and 'borrowing', and they quickly found this to be a place where they could put this art to good effect. The ground floor of the building had previously been a fish and chip shop. The equipment was still there, dirty, greasy, uncared-for, abandoned for the duration by the owners. But Fusilier Rossi, from the Regal Café in Maryhill Road, Glasgow, a café still being run in his enforced absence by his wife and daughters to the general satisfaction of its regular clientele, could see beneath the grease and grime; and what he saw brought delight to his eyes.

Off-duty times were put to good use by him and his mates. Two days later, the equipment was clean, even shining. Tables and benches had been scrubbed, rickety chairs repaired. Two fusiliers had returned from a quick foray into the countryside with two sacks of potatoes. A large can of cooking oil, thought to be unobtainable, suddenly appeared as if by magic. Contacts had quickly been made with local fishermen. There are few who are more practised in low cunning than the Lowland Scot from the Gorbals or the Cowcaddens, or more determined in their ways;

and Fusilier Rossi, proud of his adopted nationality, was no exception. On the third evening after having taken over the building, the junior subaltern, in his little look-out/bedroom in the attic could smell the unmistakable aroma of frying fish and chips wafting up the stairs. He descended to the ground floor to find the off-duty members of his platoon enjoying the best meal they had eaten for days, with a beaming Fusilier Rossi behind the counter happily loading another supply of chips into the smoking, bubbling fat in the frier. "Yours coming up in a jiffy, sir," called Rossi, "help yourself to vinegar if you want some."

For several days the platoon enjoyed the fruits of their combined capitalistic endeavours; their commander saw no need to curb their efforts, for in no way did these interfere with their military duties, and they kept morale high. In any case, he himself thoroughly enjoyed the end product, and contributed willingly to the 'kitty'. No doubt some profits were being made, but what was the harm in that? Initiative deserved its due reward. But then Fusilier Rossi's enterprise came to an abrupt end. Complaints began to reach battalion HQ from local café owners. Apparently the business had developed, unknown to the junior subaltern, and Rossi was now selling fish and chips to members of the local populace at prices which greatly undercut those of the civilian restaurants, whose supplies were limited by rationing difficulties. Battalion HQ in the person of the adjutant, made the necessary investigations, having previously been in complete ignorance of the whole affair. These resulted in a reprimand for the platoon commander, and the immediate closing down of the whole operation. This was not the disappointment that it might have seemed, as the battalion's delayed move to the north Norfolk coast took place very soon afterwards.

It was the secondary pillbox at Weybourne Hope which was instrumental in gaining for the junior subaltern his first and only official praise from Brigade. The pillbox had been erected at the foot of the slope, near the hollow which today serves as a car park. Because of its situation, it flooded easily in wet weather: this made life even more uncomfortable for the occupants. The junior subaltern decided that a drainage trench should be dug at the rear, in an attempt to divert the water away from the pillbox. His men were reluctantly engaged on this task when, unannounced, the brigadier's car, flag flying, appeared at the end of the lane which leads from the village. Calling his men to attention, he saluted the brigadier as the latter approached with his escorting officers. The brigadier, a somewhat elderly and much beribboned soldier of early vintage, surveyed the half-completed trench.

"Yours coming up in a jiffy, sir."

It was well known that he regarded with grave displeasure any extra comforts for the troops under his command. He had recently, indeed, issued an order forbidding the wearing of Balaclava helmets: "My men must learn to be tough!" What would he then think of the idea of men spending their time digging a drain, the only object of which was to improve the comfort of their pillbox? The junior subaltern awaited the seemingly inevitable explosion, only to be surprised to see the brigadier smiling at him. He was even more surprised by the ensuing remark. "Well done, boy: carry on the good work!" Another salute, and the brigadier returned to his car and drove off, leaving behind a pleased but puzzled platoon commander to complete the drainage trench.

Next day there arrived at battalion HQ a memo from Brigade, to say that the brigadier on his latest tour of inspection had been gravely displeased to find that little had been done by units to ensure the all-round protection of defence positions. Only one platoon officer (and here the junior subaltern was named) had obviously realised that enemy attack might come from the rear as well as, or instead of, frontally. This officer had shown initiative and a sound appreciation of the situation by digging alternative positions facing inland. He was to be commended.

The junior subaltern was delighted to read a copy of this memo which the adjutant had, with obvious reluctance, passed on to him. He was glad that someone appreciated his drainage trench, even if for the wrong reasons; for his men, who had dug the thing with great lack of enthusiasm, and who were at that moment standing ankle-deep in cold, muddy water in a pillbox flooded even more deeply than before, had for the previous hour been muttering their less than flattering opinions on the subject.

He read the memo again, then folded it carefully and replaced it in the pocket of his battledress blouse. He gazed out through the blanket of rain at the sullen, grey North Sea, then glanced down at his watch: only a few minutes to go until stand-down, then back to the comfort of the billet in Rose Cottage and a welcome, if hasty breakfast. He gently patted the pocket in which the brigadier's message reposed, and anticipated with no little pleasure the expression of astonishment on the face of his company commander when he handed him the memo to read. That, indeed, would be something worth seeing.

15. ABRAHAM'S BOSOM

For the first time the junior subaltern met Mac when both were attending the same OCTU course at Bulford Camp, Salisbury Plain, early in 1940. They struck up an almost immediate friendship. There was a slight air of mystery about Mac. He had enlisted as a boy soldier in the early 1930s and had worked his way up the ranks to become one the youngest sergeant-majors in the army. His performance at OCTU was outstanding. What was puzzling was his background. He did not conform to the normal pattern of a peace-time regular soldier in the ranks: he had the bearing, speech and manners of one who came from a privileged family. Mac, however, never spoke about his past; any questioning, any hinting, was at once discouraged, and he refused to be drawn on the subject.

The two men were commissioned into The Royal Scots Fusiliers on the same day (Mac had served previously in a different Scottish regiment), reported to the depot at Ayr at the same time, and had been posted together to join the 11th Battalion, then at Melton Mowbray. There, their friendship deepened. Mac, tall and strong, did not suffer fools gladly. He had very definite likes and dislikes, which he was not slow to air, and could quickly become belligerent, especially after a few drinks. He had a quick mind where military matters were concerned. He often questioned army pronouncements, which frequently appeared to him to be based on ideas more applicable to the 1914-18 war than to the present one. These traits of his character at times threatened to land him in difficulties with higher authority, but for some reason the junior subaltern was able to exert a calming and restraining influence over him when he recognised that trouble might lie ahead. Mac surprisingly accepted advice from him when he would listen to nobody else. He showed himself to be an outstanding officer, was soon promoted to captain, and assumed command of C Company when the battalion moved to Norfolk.

Although now in different companies, and of different rank, the two men still maintained their friendship. The battalion which held the Sheringham sector always had a company detached to Holkham; the company so detached had, because of its special duties, to be at full operational strength. When C Company was chosen for this, they were short of a second-in-command, and Mac's request for the junior subaltern was granted. The latter was therefore temporarily attached to fill that post.

This suited him very well. He was pleased to be with Mac again. Moreover, the Holkham posting was the most comfortable of all the defence sectors. The officers were billeted in the Victoria Hotel, close to the northern entrance gates of Holkham Hall. The hotel was still under civilian management, so the officers had all the comforts of normal hotel facilities. To help out, army rations were handed to the kitchen, and army personnel helped with some of the hotel duties. All the bedrooms were occupied by the officers, but the bar was open still to the locals. Other ranks were billeted in the cottages formerly used as an annexe to the hotel.

The defence duties were also different from those in the other coastal sectors. Holkham Bay is wide but comparatively shallow. The tide ebbs and flows quickly, goes out a long way, exposing a vast area of sand. To the landward side of the dunes there is a long, narrow wood consisting mainly of pine trees. Because of the shallowness of the bay, it was considered to be an unlikely place for any large invasion attempt; but on the other hand, these same conditions made it a very possible choice for the landing of individuals or small parties in vessels of little draught. The trees would offer immediate concealment. Orders were given that, should any such landings be intercepted, then every effort was to be made to capture the intruders alive. They would be most valuable for intelligence purposes.

To implement this policy, emphasis was placed on regular and frequent patrolling of the area, rather than on static defence positions. Patrols when off duty spent their time in a large nissen hut in the woods, close to the beach at the end of the narrow road, Lady Anne's Drive, which led down from the hotel. One end of the patrolled area culminated at the point where the navigable channel from Wells harbour meets the sea. Here a minor road ran along the sea wall. In the woods, just off the road, was a cluster of huts and chalets around a small inland pool, used in peace time as a boating pond. According to a faded noticeboard, this little complex went under the name of Abraham's

Bosom. There was no obvious reason for such a title; the troops made ribald jokes about it. What any intruding German would make of it was anybody's guess. The huts and chalets were all locked, with windows shuttered; the place had a desolate air.

Throughout the whole area at that time resident civilians were restricted in their movements, and visitors were prohibited. This prohibition applied also to wives and girl friends of the troops. Some of the more senior officers managed to circumvent this regulation and to install their wives in rented property. Those of lower rank were not so fortunate. This was one of the army orders which Mac decided to ignore. Twice he had been reprimanded for breaking the restriction: he had been warned that a third offence might result in a court martial, with serious consequences to his military career.

For a while he had shown uneasy restraint. Caution, however, was foreign to Mac's nature. He had developed a close relationship with a girl from one of the big hunting families near Melton Mowbray when the battalion had been stationed there, and he was determined to continue this. The junior subaltern was therefore not very surprised to be told by him that he had found a way to have Peggy installed nearby for a few days without anyone else being any the wiser. The door of one of the chalets at Abraham's Bosom had a lock which, he found, responded to one of his own keys. It was an ideal place; out of the way, and could be made comfortable. Essential services, for some reason, had not been cut off. Even the telephone was working. Peggy could stay there quite happily for a few days without anyone else being aware of her presence in the area, except of course for the junior subaltern, who could help by ensuring that the duty patrols did not include Abraham's Bosom on their routes during the vital times. He could also warn Mac on the telephone should any crisis develop. The former, cautious by nature and by inclination, did not like the idea, and said so; but Mac's mind was made up, and he could be more stubborn than the proverbial mule when he so chose.

On the first occasion all went well. Peggy, who was working with the American Ambulance in Nottingham, came and went unobserved. All officers had a door key to the hotel, so Mac could slip in unobserved sometime before dawn. Then one Monday morning, at about 3 am, the junior subaltern was woken by Mac's voice in his ear. He switched on his bedside lamp. Mac was standing there, his usually immaculate uniform mud-stained, with one sleeve of his tunic torn. Blood was oozing from a cut beside one eye, and running down his cheek. His face was smeared with dirt, and there was what looked like a mixture of mud and blood on his collar.

Before his friend could speak, Mac whispered, "Don't say anything – just listen: please do as I tell you, or I'll be in big trouble. Something's happened, too complicated to explain, and I haven't time. But I've got to do two things fast: get Peggy away from here as quickly as possible; and go back to the chalet to remove all our traces. I can't do both by myself, you've got to help. Don't ask questions: the less you know the better." Whilst the junior subaltern hurriedly dressed, his company commander explained what he wanted done. "The PU is out in the road. Peggy's in it. Drive her to Fakenham, drop her off at the station where her car is parked, and get back here as soon as you can. I'll answer for you if necessary. Just hope to God the balloon doesn't go up in the next two hours." Whilst giving these instructions Mac had managed to remove the mess from his hands, face and uniform at the wash-hand basin. He covered the cut on his forehead with an elastoplast dressing, and, discarding his tunic, borrowed a spare battledress blouse from the junior subaltern. The latter's further attempts to find out more were brusquely cut short by the reiteration that the less he knew the better, and Mac led him quietly down the stairs and out through the back door. The company truck was parked under some trees close to the park gates. As the two men approached, Peggy got out. She and Mac exchanged a few words and a quick embrace, whilst the junior subaltern started up the engine. Peggy resumed her seat in the front. Mac clambered over the tail-board at the rear of the PU, with a request to drop him off at the crossroads on the outskirts of Wells.

Once on the road to Fakenham, the driver had time to collect his rather muddled thoughts. So much had happened so quickly. He had met Peggy on only a few previous occasions, and knew little about her, but she seemed to have remained remarkably composed. She had not spoken since they had left Mac near Wells. He now ventured a question, but she was as reticent as Mac had been, repeating only that she could help best by saying nothing; nobody must know that she had been staying in the chalet. Once Mac had finished, there would be no trace that it had ever been used by them. Perhaps he would explain more later, when all this had blown over. The junior subaltern respected her wishes, and asked no further questions; they continued the journey in silence, making good time along the traffic-free roads. He turned off into the station yard at Fakenham, and drew up alongside the only car parked there, a small MG. Peggy got out, collected a canvas grip from the back of the PU and, with a few words of thanks, climbed into her car and drove off. He, still greatly wondering, drove back to Holkham, arriving in good time to return unseen to his room, and to appear at breakfast as if nothing untoward had happened. He was relieved to see that Mac was already at the table, meticulously turned-out as usual, with only a small plaster over his right eye-brow to remind him of the strange events of the night just past.

There was no chance of any private conversation until that evening. The junior subaltern was naturally more than anxious to hear Mac's explanation; but he was disappointed. All that he was told was that everything was under control. Peggy had reached home safely, the chalet was now 'out', and "last night never happened." He tried to elicit further information, but Mac was not to be drawn. At least, there would be no further worries about chalet arrangements; he had never shared his company commander's confidence about their infallibility. He must be content with that blessing.

Some days later a small and badly damaged inflatable dingy was washed ashore in Wells harbour. An immediate search of the area was ordered, and extra patrols arranged. Near the point, on rocks at the base of the sea wall, was found the body of a dead man, dressed in civilian clothes. The battalion intelligence officer was called to the scene, who quickly established that some of the documents found in the man's pockets were false. The spectacle case which he carried was made by a well-known German firm. Further search of the immediate area disclosed a flick-knife of a type known to be favoured by German intruders. His wallet contained bank notes which, on checking, proved to be forgeries. All evidence pointed to his having been an enemy agent. A few nights earlier there had been a sudden and unexpected storm. It was presumed that the man, attempting to land, had been driven off course and on to the rocks. Then, attempting to scale the sea-wall, he had fallen back into the sea. The fall must have been fatal, for although he had been in the water, death had not been by drowning. There were injuries on his body consistent with having been dashed against the rocks by the force of strong waves. The investigation ended, reports to higher authority were submitted. Patrols were ordered to be extra vigilant.

Authority was satisfied with the conclusion reached by the investigation. The junior subaltern was less certain. Peggy had said little on their journey to Fakenham, but one remark that she had made stuck in his mind. She had said that, if the circumstances had been different,

Mac might have earned a medal for his conduct that night. She had not added to the remark, saying she had already said too much: but it made the junior subaltern think very hard. He had no absolute means of knowing the truth of what had occurred that night at Abraham's Bosom, but he was certain in his own mind there must be a direct link between the events there, in or near the chalet, and the discovery of the dead man only a few hundred yards away.

It did not take much imagination to visualise what would have happened if Mac either then, or on the way there or back, had come upon a German intruder. To obey orders, to take the man prisoner, to hand him over for questioning; these correct actions would have led to all his arrangements about the use of the chalet being exposed, with certain damage to all his service ambitions. Such a man in that area, ideal for concealment, was an obvious threat to Peggy herself: he might well have made use of the seclusion of Abraham's Bosom as a safe place from which to operate. Mac, impulsive, strong, an expert in unarmed combat, fearful of Peggy's safety, would not have hesitated, would have acted instinctively. After his experiences in France he had no love for the Germans. Mac would have taken the only course open to him.

All the evidence available to the junior subaltern, and the events in which he himself had become involved, pointed that way. The discovery of the body, apparently washed up on the rocks only a short distance from Abraham's Bosom, was the natural and logical outcome. He had no proof, nor did he seek any, but there were just too many coincidences for him privately to accept the official findings, remembering as he did the events of that night. Everything had worked out satisfactorily. The authorities were satisfied, the chalet was safely locked and securely barred once more. Peggy had not been compromised. Mac's career was not in jeopardy. And if his own interpretation was correct, a German agent had been foiled. Let the matter rest there.

C Company's duties at Holkham came to an end, and with them the attachment of its second-in-command, who returned to his former position in B Company. The incident faded into insignificance as the greater events of the war unfolded. During the next eighteen months first Mac, and then the junior subaltern, left the battalion to join different units overseas, never to meet again. The latter returned to Wells several years after the end of the war, to see if Chalet No. 3 still stood in the wood beside the boating lake. He could not find it, it had either been removed, or had been so transformed as to be unrecognisable. He gazed at the holiday complex, at the happy seaside visitors, at the scene so very different from before, and could not help but wonder. What were Mac's only words on the events of that night so long ago? "Last night never happened." Perhaps Mac had been right, it had been only a dream. But if not, if something violent did happen then its secrets, with the answers to so many questions, remained hidden safely within the confines of Abraham's Bosom, amongst the tall pine trees on the sandy verge of Holkham Bay.

16. THINGS THAT GO BUMP

It has been said that war consists of long periods of boredom interrupted by short periods of intense fear. For a soldier in the front line on the north Norfolk coast there was plenty of the former, but fortunately little of the latter. It was a time of waiting, waiting for the invasion that all thought was bound to come; much of that waiting was indeed boring, and often very uncomfortable. No one in his right senses would enjoy standing night after night on Weybourne Hope in winter's weather, or patrolling the Salthouse marshes in the teeth of a howling blizzard. There were more pleasant things to do than to wrestle with coils of barbed wire, to dig trenches, to lay mines, to make Molotov cocktails, to argue with farmers annoyed by military interference; but such things were all essential at the time.

There was boredom, there was discomfort, there were worries about what lay ahead: and there were also, indeed some moments of danger and yes, fear. Until the so-called Baedeker raids in 1942, enemy action tended to be limited and sporadic, affecting only a few; but for these few there were frightening occasions. Enemy aircraft liked to make sudden, low-level attacks, singly or in pairs, on forward positions during daylight hours when men were working on the defences. The fusiliers of 11 Platoon were renowned neither for speed of thought nor for quickness of movement, but they showed both when, perched 12 feet up one morning on the top of scaffolding near Robin's Friend, a Messerschmit suddenly dived at them out of the sun, its machine guns blazing. The occasional bomb was dropped at night. Sometimes such an attack would set off a mine on the beach, or in one of the other defensive mine-fields. This often resulted in the sympathetic detonation of other mines, with noisy and spectacular results; not popular, as of course it meant that the field had to be relaid.

The pillbox at the top of Beeston Hump had been carelessly sited and poorly constructed. What is more, it was all too visible. Possibly because of this, it was frequently the object of attack by enemy aircraft. The gun embrasures were too wide and incorrectly placed, so were easily penetrated by bullets which then ricocheted wildly around the interior like a swarm of angry bees, to the great discomforture of the occupants. On two occasions men had been wounded in this way. Troops on duty therefore preferred to take cover in the slit trenches dug within the position rather than inside the pillbox, against which the fury of the enemy aircraft was invariably directed.

One day, when 11 Platoon was on duty on Beeston Hump, a Messerschmit seemed to take a particular dislike to this pillbox. The day was hot and sunny. The men resting after some tiring and tedious work on the barbed wire were relaxing and making the most of the pleasant summer conditions. Suddenly an enemy fighter was seen approaching at speed, low over the sea. Most of the men leapt into the slit trenches. Three others, who had been sunning themselves further away, dressed only in their underpants, were too far off to avail themselves of that protection. They rushed for the shelter of the pillbox wall on the landward side, keeping it between themselves and the enemy. They reached safety just as the first blast of machine gun fire hit the front of the pillbox. The plane roared overhead, banked steeply, and came speeding in from the opposite direction to resume its attack. The three men, preferring from previous experience not to seek refuge within the box, had just time enough to run round it to gain the protection of the opposite wall.

This somewhat bizarre quadrille was repeated several times, and continued for two or three minutes. The friends of the unfortunate men, realising that they themselves were out of harm's way in their trench, and their mates were in no real danger, applauded each circuit loudly, shouting encouragement and making various improper suggestions to the scantily dressed participants. Then the German, having expended a considerable amount of ammunition without result, tired of the game, gave the pillbox one last, vicious burst, and headed out to sea. The junior subaltern, who had watched the proceedings from his small dug-out HQ, and who had obeyed with some reluctance the order then in force not to engage the enemy with small-arms fire so as to preserve precious ammunition, was slightly dismayed by the non-appearance of any RAF 'planes during the encounter. However, the Battle of Britain was in full swing, so no doubt they were more profitably engaged elsewhere at the time.

The odd bomb was dropped; machine gun attacks were made by

Three others, who had been sunning themselves dressed only in their underpants... rushed for the shelter of the pillbox wall...

enemy aircraft on military targets and on towns and villages along the coast, causing some casualties and damage. All this was expected and accepted as the normal hazard and fortunes of war. Much greater anger and concern was aroused by the dropping of different kinds of booby traps. Such unpleasant devices may be justified on the battlefield, where soldiers alone can be victims. But here, on the Norfolk coast, civilians and even children were at risk. The first indication that the enemy were using these booby traps came when a young courting couple, walking on the heath above Salthouse, noticed a bright blue fountain pen lying on the path. The youth picked it up, and began to unscrew the cap. The ensuing explosion removed three fingers of one hand, and left him blind in one eye. His companion escaped with lesser injuries and shock. Despite repeated public warnings, others came to grief on similar devices.

All the booby traps were designed to look attractive: brightly coloured pens and pencils, pencil cases, watches, notebooks with enticing covers, cigarette cases, matchboxes. The natural instinct on seeing one of these lying on the ground was to pick it up: warnings were easily forgotten for the immediate instant. These objects were dropped haphazardly, and over a wide area. One little girl, playing in her garden in a village near Holt, saw what looked to her like a small parcel, wrapped in Christmas paper, entangled in the branches of a tree. She tried to tug it free, and it exploded in her face.

Two fusiliers, hoping to earn some easy money by the sale of souvenirs, and believing that they had sufficient knowledge about explosive devices, disobeyed orders and began to collect these objects and to sell them, having of course first defused and rendered them harmless. They should have known better. One day they found a pen on the promenade in Sheringham. All similar discoveries which they had carefully defused previously had screw-caps with left-hand threads. This one, unfortunately for them, was fitted with a right-hand thread. After a lengthy spell in hospital, both received court-martial sentences. All in all, an unrewarding enterprise for them both.

These booby traps, indiscriminate in their effects, did little to serve the German cause. Their material value was minimal, and they certainly reinforced the determination of the East Anglian populace, civilian and military, to resist anything that the enemy might throw at them.

Troops on the coast were constantly being reminded of the need to be vigilant against any attempt made by enemy agents to land in the remote areas. There was also the possibility of sudden, snap raids. The RSF experienced none of the latter, though the other two battalions of the brigade were said to have been engaged in some minor incidents, with which they had dealt successfully. Three agents were caught within a few hours of coming ashore near Stiffkey, and were, as was revealed in later years, converted to act as double agents, to the British advantage, for the remainder of the war.

The junior subaltern and members of his platoon had, as it were, the best front seats to watch an interesting little incident which took place at sea just off West Runton. A small British coaster, making its steady way northwards, was attacked simultaneously by a German E-boat (a fast motor-boat) and an enemy aircraft. It quickly raised its barrage balloon, and brought its little pom-pom gun into action. The odds against it were soon reversed by the appearance of three Hurricanes, which resulted in the speedy withdrawal of the foe.

Resuming its voyage, apparently unscathed, the coaster left its anti-aircraft balloon aloft. Black storm clouds had been gathering all afternoon. There was a sudden clap of thunder. A vivid flash of lightning struck the balloon, which promptly burst into flames and disintegrated. Men could be seen on deck hauling in the now useless cable to which the balloon had been attached: the lightning, running down the cable, must have started a fire on board, for black smoke could be seen rising from amidships. The junior subaltern used his field telephone to inform his HQ of this, although already rescue craft were reported to be on their way. These did not remain long with the coaster. The fire must have been a minor one, easily extinguished, for soon the victim had resumed her solitary voyage.

As he watched the vessel disappear into the distance, the thought occurred to him, that fortune perhaps did not always favour the brave. The coaster and her crew had stoutly defied the enemy and had, with the help of the Hurricanes, repelled the attack, only to have been rudely struck by an actual bolt from the blue. Hardly a just reward for their brave action. Recently, he remembered, both the German and the British leaders had been claiming divine support for their respective causes. This incident made him rather wonder which claim was the correct one, and which side had first call upon divine Providence.

17. PUBLIC RELATIONS

Oak Wood stands on a small hill beside the Sheringham to Blakeney road, not far from Weybourne. The soldiers of 11 Platoon were camped in a clearing near the centre of the wood, beside a rough path which led down to the main road. Close to the junction of path and road, surrounded and overhung by trees, stood a small and dilapidated cottage, the chimney of which, even in summer time, seemed continuously to be belching thick smoke. As a result, the cottage was often partially concealed by an acrid fog; the dense, overhanging foliage prevented much dispersal except on very windy days.

This cottage was inhabited by a strange couple of indeterminate age. Man and wife were always muffled up in long coats and scarves, whatever the weather, both with faces wizened and of a brownish colour, no doubt due to their smoke-related surroundings. Indeed, they were quickly named 'the Kippers' by the troops. Outside the cottage, in a rough clearing, was a hen run. This was often empty, for the chicken wire surrounding the enclosure was in a poor state of repair, and the hens wandered at will. Today they would certainly have deserved the appellation of 'free-range poultry'.

Hens of course, mean eggs; eggs are food; and food was a subject always much in the minds of 11 Platoon. It was not surprising, therefore, that some of the fusiliers soon established contact with the occupants of the cottage. As the soldiers in the main spoke broad Glaswegian, and the couple equally broad Norfolk, the junior subaltern marvelled at the quick establishment of understanding. Knowing well the habits of his platoon members, and fearing that they might have illegal designs on the errant poultry, he decided to anticipate possible trouble by warning his men against any attempt to try to 'liberate' either hens or eggs. He was immediately assured by recently-promoted Lance Corporal Rossi, the entrepeneur Italian-Scot from Maryhill. that there was no danger of this. He and some of his mates had already come to a firm understanding with the Greens – as the couple were rather incongruously named – and woe betide any man who did anything to disrupt such arrangements. The platoon commander refrained from asking what these involved, being quite happy to let the situation rest. In any case, the terms of the agreement made between cottage and platoon soon became evident; the dilapidated chicken fence was repaired with wire which, on closer inspection, might have revealed a military origin; a smart new chicken coop appeared, as if by magic; the enclosure was tidied up, and gravel spread. Coincidental with all this, the rather monotonous platoon breakfasts suddenly became much more inviting, with fried eggs on the menu several times a week.

This happy state of affairs continued for some time, until one day the junior subaltern was approached by Lance Corporal Rossi. The latter was very perturbed. The Kippers (the Greens) had told him that some of their hens had been stolen, by the RSF, they alleged. The agreement was in danger of being cancelled. He – Rossi – had been making vigorous investigations within the platoon, but in vain: no clues as to the culprits. Indeed, he was pretty sure nobody in 11 Platoon was involved. Would the officer please go to see the Kippers and have the matter cleared up? If it wasn't, then no more eggs – "even for the officers".

That evening the junior subaltern penetrated the fog which permanently enveloped the cottage, and knocked at the split, stable-type door. Mr Green appeared and, the reason for his mission having been explained, he was invited in. Mrs Green, aproned, with bonnet on head and the usual bedroom slippers (worn indoors and out) on her feet, was attending to a large, wood-burning range, the obvious source of the perpetual smoke. The furniture was basic: a table, two wooden chairs, a dilapidated couch and an old arm chair. In a recess was a large bed. Alongside the range was a sink, with a dripping cold water tap, and a few shelves on which stood some crockery and cooking utensils. The smoke emanating from the range was reinforced by that from Mr Green's stubby clay pipe.

Invited to be seated in the old arm chair which creaked ominously under his weight, the visitor listened to Mr Green's complaint. As by then he had been in the area for some months, the junior subaltern was able to understand most of what was being said. It was as Rossi had indicated: several hens had disappeared in the night. The new fence was intact, so they had not strayed. No trace of feathers, so no predatory animals involved. The only people around were the RSF soldiers, therefore they must have been responsible. The junior subaltern refuted this allegation, but promised to investigate. He then departed as soon as he could, eyes streaming from the effects of the smoke, the heat of the room and the attempts to suppress his desire to cough.

Back in camp, he called a platoon meeting. This convinced him that Rossi was right in his assertion that nobody there was to blame. 11 Platoon were no saints, and they would without hesitation appropriate things whenever they could, when such action was to their individual or corporate benefit. But in this case, no. In the first place, they all stood to lose; in the second, they would not risk bringing down upon themselves the wrath of their fellow fusiliers, and especially that of Rossi, who was respected and feared for reasons other than his slight military rank. Members of his pre-war Maryhill razor-gang were still with him in the battalion, and it was more than unwise to trifle with them.

It was generally agreed that to preserve the good name of the platoon and, perhaps more importantly, their source of fresh eggs, greater security measures should be taken and, if possible, the culprits caught. The following day the hen run was surrounded with some 'spare' army dannert barbed wire. A single trip-wire was pegged down, to which were attached at intervals empty tins and cans. They did not have long to wait for results. That very night, at about 2 am there was a loud rattle. The two fusiliers on watch, shouting to awake the rest of the platoon, rushed down the hill to investigate. There they found a furious Mrs Green trying to disentangle herself from a coil of wire, the empty tins still jangling noisily around her. The end of the wire had been attached to the wall of the outside privy. Mrs Green, on a nocturnal visit, had deviated from the direct route, and had enmeshed herself. Her vocabulary showed a width and expressiveness not previously in evidence; she was by nature taciturn. With some difficulty the soldiers eased her from the wire, and she withdrew to the cottage, still muttering. Of her husband, there was no sign. First thing next morning, under Rossi's direction, the wire was re-sited so that in future Mrs Green might safely walk.

Several nights later, the junior subaltern was rudely awoken by a tremendous clamour: shouting, clattering of cans, cackling of hens, even the barking of dogs presumably from the farm house about half a mile away. Together with most of the platoon he ran down the path to the cottage. There, illuminated by the light of several torches held by fusiliers, he found the cause of the disturbance. Enmeshed in the concertina wire were two men, swearing volubly. Close by stood the two 11 Platoon sentries, rifles pointed at the intruders: beside them the Greens, Mr Green speaking rapidly and unintelligibly, Mrs Green giving vent to high-pitched screams. Within the enclosure, the agitated hens were flapping around, cackling incessantly.

Loud blasts on his whistle restored comparative calm and order (the hens continued to protest, and Mrs Green's silence could only be temporary). The junior subaltern then told Rossi and two others to free the men from the wire. The two intruders, faces and hands scratched and bleeding from the barbs, were obviously in a state of fear, and made little attempt to defend themselves when questioned. Their badges were those of the Royal Artillery, and they freely admitted that they were stationed at the nearby Weybourne AA camp, and that they had been on a previous occasion to steal both hens and eggs.

The junior subaltern gave them a thorough verbal blasting, at the same time making up his mind what should be done with the miscreants. To put them under arrest, and hold them until the Military Police arrived, would be the correct procedure. But that would involve various complications: paper work, witnesses, court-martial and a possible court case as well. Much wasted time. What was important to him and to 11 Platoon was that they had been cleared, in the eyes of the Greens, of all suspicion of hen-stealing. The former amicable arrangements could be restored. He would return the two men to their camp escorted by Rossi and his section, with orders to leave them at the camp gates. What happened to them on the way was up to Rossi, who, when annoyed, was not devoid of unpleasant ideas. The men had presumably broken out of camp; they would just have to break in again. Rossi would know not to overdo any nasty tricks.

Carefully instructed, the lance corporal and his men marched off into the night with the two gunners. 11 Platoon and their commander, the Greens, and the startled and still clucking hens retired to their respective beds. Next morning, when Percival awoke his platoon officer with his cup of gunfire tea, the pleasant aroma of frying eggs and bacon once more gave promise of a tasty breakfast.

The north Norfolk coast was a restricted area, and many civilians had moved elsewhere; but of course a large number still remained. Relations between the latter and the troops at that time were usually good. Both realised that at any moment they might find themselves engulfed in battle; but this eventuality was probably more difficult to contemplate for the civilians than for the military. It must have been hard to visualise street fighting around the house in which one had lived

Enmeshed in the concertina wire were two men swearing volubly.

all one's life, or to imagine a pitched battle on the fairways of one's own golf course. The junior subaltern at times worried about what would happen when the invasion came (to the civilians the governing word was 'if', to the soldiers it was 'when'). There was an official evacuation policy, but a vague one. What would happen, for instance, to the families of members of the Home Guard? Would there be the time, would there be the transport? In any event, happenings in France, vividly described by those members of the battalion who had served there, proved that the Germans would attack all road and rail movements from the air. He was not the only one to have worries on that score.

Not surprisingly, there was some friction at times between civilians and troops. The army had been told to be sympathetic to all the needs and wishes of the civilian population. The army was also required urgently to establish and maintain the best possible defence system with the rather meagre and inadequate resources at its disposal. These two instructions were often mutually contradictory. The most suitable site for a pillbox might be in the middle of a cornfield. The farmer would object strongly: he was being exhorted by the government to grow as much grain as he could. Lanes leading from the beaches could best be denied to an invading enemy by the laying of land mines; but the fishermen, urged by the same government to provide as much fish as possible, needed this access to their boats and to the sea. And so there were disagreements. Committees were formed, compromises reached; but wars are not won by committees nor by compromises, and at times angry words were exchanged. Nevertheless the troops of the RSF and the inhabitants of the north Norfolk coast overcame most of the problems that arose. The soldiers enjoyed the generous hospitality so often extended to them; the civilians, understanding the situation, made them welcome and put up with their inconvenient presence.

All those who served in that area during these early war years must have retained special memories of certain East Anglians with whom they came in contact. The junior subaltern was no exception. For various and very different reasons he still readily recalls, 50 years later, the Taylors in their home on Beeston Hump, Ben, the taxi-driver cum undertaker in Holt, Mrs Banks and her strange lights, and many others; of the latter, there were two who stand out in his memory with especial clarity; Mrs Alice Beaton, owner of a tiny shop in Blakeney, and Mrs Betty Goldsmith, one of the ladies who dispensed refreshments from her van in Salthouse, come rain, shine or high water.

Mrs Beaton, a middle-aged widow, kept a little tobacco and sweet shop situated half way down the main street in Blakeney. There was never anything to be seen on display in the small, curved front window; few customers seemed to patronise the shop. One day the junior subaltern, having a few sweet coupons left over from his leave, decided to try to cash them for any chocolate or other luxury she might have. Ducking his head, he squeezed through the little door; as it shut behind him a bell tinkled, and Mrs Beaton, reluctantly it seemed, emerged from a back room through a curtain which divided it from the main shop. She was sorry, no, she had no chocolates or other sweets. She did have a few cigarettes somewhere; would he like them? She rummaged in a drawer and produced several packets of Gold Flake, for which he proffered a pound note. The change she gave him was too much; he pointed this out. No, it wasn't. These were old stock, the change was correct. Anyway, she couldn't be doing with all these coupons and forms and regulations; she would be giving up the business, she just couldn't cope. She didn't know what she was going to do.

She was obviously in the depths of despair, which struck the junior subaltern as being very sad, for she was a gentle, kind person, obviously overwhelmed by the loss of her husband and by the intricacies imposed by war-time regulations. He tried to encourage her by telling her that hers was the only shop of its kind surviving in the village; it could still provide a living. No, she couldn't manage. Then he had a brainwave: would she continue if he found her some capable help? She considered. Well, that would be kind: she would try. So the junior subaltern returned to the company office and made some private arrangements with the B Company clerk, Lance Corporal McClure, himself a shopkeeper before the army claimed him. On the next free evening they returned to the shop. There they found enough in the way of old coupons and certificates to convince McClure that the shop could easily be restocked; indeed, it could be very well stocked and then easily maintained. It was obvious that this was going to be a project dear to McClure's heart, and that everything could safely be left in his capable hands. As company clerk, he had more free time than most, so that would be no problem. There was no need for Captain Smith to know about the arrangements. By the time the two men had left the shop, Mrs Beaton was already more cheerful.

His confidence was not misplaced. Within 10 days the shop window was resplendent with goods arranged proudly by McClure himself. Inside, the walls freshly painted, the counter gleaming, the shelves were stocked with sweets, chocolate and cigarettes; no one need know that when the company truck had visited Norwich on official business it had made a slight, unofficial detour. Under McClure's tutelage, Mrs Beaton soon grasped the workings of the regulations and also, perhaps unwittingly, how to circumvent some of them. Her shop, ignored before, was now a magnet in the village; she herself looked years younger. Six months later she became Mrs McClure. Rationing was more stringent, cigarettes, tobacco and sweets were more difficult to find; but there was always something under the counter for the junior subaltern at 'Beaton's'.

Betty Goldsmith was a large, purposeful, jovial lady who, with an assistant, brought the WVS van to Salthouse to dispense welcome cups of tea and other goodies to the troops working there on the defences. Even on those days when the weather was at its worst – and that, at Salthouse, can be really something – she was always entertainingly cheerful. She could be determined, too, as she showed when the brigadier restricted the morning break, so that her 'Jocks', working further up the village and on the saltmarshes, did not have enough time to enjoy the village bakery's hot muffins and the WVS refreshments. She was furious, and showed it. But more: she converted her fury into action.

The junior subaltern learnt the whole story from a friend of his on the brigade staff. Mrs Goldsmith arrived at the HQ gates in her own car, ignored completely the sentry's challenge and signal to stop, and drove straight up the drive to park in a space marked 'Officers Only'. She then advanced briskly on the main entrance door, answered the sentry's challenge by replying "Idiot, you know who I am", (she frequently visited the HQ on WVS business) and left the poor man bewildered and speechless. At the reception desk she requested very firmly to be taken to the brigadier. To the ATS sergeant's enquiry as to whether she had arranged an appointment she made a most unladylike reply, turned about, strode over to the brigadier's office, marched inside, and slammed the door behind her. The astonished listeners in the hall heard the sound of raised voices. Then, after a few minutes, Mrs Goldsmith emerged, a satisfied look on her face, returned to her car, and sped off at a furious pace, scattering gravel generously over an incoming squad of soldiers. The next day it was announced in Part I orders that the morning break for all soldiers working on defences was to be restored forthwith to its former length, 'by orders of the brigadier'.

As the junior subaltern's friend observed later, when describing the event, "After Mrs Goldsmith, who can now fear the Hun?"

18. VERY IMPORTANT PERSONS

Visitations by VIPs were never viewed with much enthusiasm by the troops. Such occasions involved extra work; often prized leisure time was lost, and normal duties were disrupted.

VIPs might be divided into two distinct groups: internal and external. The former consisted of the senior officers of Brigade or Division who would appear, usually but not always unannounced, to inspect what the men under their command were or were not doing. Of these, the one most often seen by The Royal Scots Fusiliers was the brigadier, who tended to materialise at inopportune moments, and whose visits were often followed by major or minor 'rockets', depending on the degree of displeasure which he felt. He had the nasty habit of arriving unexpectedly just at the end of the morning or evening 'stand-to'. Most of the infantry officers looked upon these 'stand-to's' as being unnecessary, and in bad weather they were often tempted to order the stand-down some minutes early. The brigadier was very fierce about this, and junior officers were well advised to avoid his displeasure. Some forward positions were safer than others in that the approach routes could be watched, and the arrival of the brigadier's car anticipated.

The junior subaltern was one of the few of such insignificant rank ever to receive official commendation from him, on that fortunate occasion when the brigadier misunderstood the reason for the digging by 11 Platoon of a trench at the rear of their frequently waterlogged pillbox (See Chapter 14). Thereafter, the brigadier made fewer visitations to 11 Platoon, no doubt having formed a good, if erroneous, opinion of that unit's efficiency.

Very set in his ways, the brigadier was inclined to keep to regular schedules. Whenever a battalion took up its tour of duty in the Blakeney sector, the CO knew that he would have one official and previously notified visit of inspection from the brigade commander. The latter would ask for a formal ceremonial parade in the grounds of the officers' mess, a large house called The White Gables. In the middle of the inspection he would suddenly announce some imaginary crisis, to see how the officers and men would respond. Knowing that the brigadier tended not to be very innovative, the CO of the RSF consulted his opposite number in the Leicesters, from whom he had recently taken over, about details of the brigadier's current thinking, and had made his plans accordingly. The selected D Company was able to carry out a complete rehearsal. Sure enough, all went as forecast by the outgoing Leicester CO. The RSF responded well to the 'surprise' crisis, and the brigadier was duly impressed.

Very different was a visit made by Marshal of the Royal Air Force Viscount Trenchard, at that time Colonel-in-Chief of the RSF whose 1st Battalion he had commanded in the 1914-18 war prior to transfer to the Royal Flying Corps. At his own request there was to be no ceremonial parade; his wish was to cause the least possible disturbance to normal duties. He wanted to visit informally, and to have a few minutes' chat with every platoon in the battalion wherever that platoon happened to be. 11 Platoon was then with B Company in Weybourne, with forward positions on the Hope and billets in the village. Arrangements were made to allow Lord Trenchard to meet the men outside the row of cottages they were occupying. He arrived without fuss in his PU, accompanied only by his driver, acknowledged the platoon's salute, then asked them to sit down wherever they could. He himself leant against the flint wall of one of the cottage gardens. A few passers-by, curious to see what was afoot, stopped to watch and were also invited to sit.

Lord Trenchard then spoke to them in simple terms, using words which are perhaps now considered old-fashioned such as 'duty' and 'loyalty'. They were all, civilians and soldiers, together in the front line. The enemy were poised to invade, and East Anglia was a likely target. After the disasters in France, there were some who voiced the opinion that the German army was invincible. Not so. They were certainly good soldiers, well equipped; but we had beaten them before, and would do so again, though this time it might take a while longer before victory was achieved. He reminded them of the old couplet 'He that would old England win, must at Weybourne Hope begin.' No better soldiers could have been chosen to defend this vital spot than The Royal Scots Fusiliers. He was sorry that they were still so short of necessary arms and equipment, but men and women all over Britain were now working day and night to rectify this. He concluded by saying that he regretted being unable to stay longer with them, but they would understand he had many others still to see. Wishing them good luck, he departed as quickly and as informally as he had arrived, his short visit having done more to boost morale than all the other, longer and formal VIP ceremonies to which they had been subjected.

One day Captain Smith, B Company commander, called an officers' meeting at which he announced that he had been instructed to provide a guard of honour to welcome the arrival of an important Free French delegation at Sheringham Station. 11 Platoon, being the 'rest' platoon on the appropriate date, would provide that guard under his command. 11 Platoon received the news with something less than enthusiasm. Not only did it mean the loss of their rest day; it also entailed a great deal of spit and polish for – in the opinion of the platoon – "a lot of bloody frogs". The junior subaltern, whilst privately sharing their sentiments, did his best to arouse and encourage a more francophile attitude amongst his men, with singular lack of success. Nevertheless, 11 Platoon, when the day came, rose as usual to the occasion; and when they paraded on the platform of Sheringham station they looked considerably smarter than they had done for many months. Even the company commander was constrained to make some unaccustomed complimentary remarks.

The Midland and Great Northern Railway train puffed into the station, locomotive bedecked with two tri-colour flags. A much-decorated, smartly uniformed French general descended, followed by a small group of aides. 11 Platoon presented arms, Captain Smith saluted. The piper launched into what for one awful moment sounded as if it were a bag-pipe adaptation of The Marseillaise, but which developed into Corporal Macewen's version of Heilan' Laddie. A few civilians, gathered on the road bridge, raised a hesitant cheer. The general and his entourage advanced to carry out the routine inspection. As the French leader stopped for a few brief words with Captain Smith, the junior subaltern's attention was attracted by one of the aides, a tall young officer sporting a neat, pointed beard and generous side-burns. There was something strangely familiar about his face, and the way he stood. Of whom did he remind him? Then it clicked: Eric Collier, a fellow RSF officer, that's who the Frenchman resembled.

Thoughts rampaged through the junior subaltern's mind. Eric was on leave. Eric was a keen practical joker. Eric disapproved of ceremonial. Eric had been a pupil at Fettes, where his housemaster was Ian Hay, the author. One of the latter's stories much admired by Eric, featured a group of students who, for a wager, had dressed up in Arab attire and had completely deceived the senior common room of an Oxford college, whose members had received them as representative of an important Middle East delegation. Quite undetected and unsuspected, they had been given an official welcome, had been wined and dined, and finally had been seen off by the master of the college himself. They had won their bet. It would be just like Eric to try a similar prank. He looked again at the French lieutenant, more closely this time. Was that Eric's face behind the handsome beard? Why was the officer wearing dark glasses? Was the whole affair a complete hoax?

The general and his entourage moved slowly along the ranks of 11 Platoon, stopping occasionally to speak to individual soldiers. At one stage the aide who was of special interest to the junior subaltern stopped immediately in front of him. He was almost certain it was Eric. "You stupid idiot," he hissed, "you'll never get away with this!" The aide looked at him questioningly, but not batting an eyelid, then muttered something which sounded like, "Oh, come on!" The junior subaltern could not but admire his friend's coolness, and the very professional way in which the whole of the French party was behaving. He was sorely tempted to give a sharp tug to Eric's false beard, but he dared not expose the hoax. It deserved success. In any case, if the perpetrators were discovered, there would be all hell to pay. Captain Smith would go beserk, and that would only be the start of Eric's troubles. The consequences would be dire. Temptation anyhow was removed as the inspecting officers moved on to complete the ceremony.

More salutes, then the Frenchmen left the station to board two large black Rolls Royce limousines, one of which was being driven by Ben, the taxi-driver cum undertaker from Holt. "Will ye no come back again?" inquired Corporal Macewen on his pipes. The group of civilians, now increased in numbers by members of the Dormy Hotel staff, waved and cheered. The two cars, flags fluttering, crossed the bridge and sped out of sight. 11 Platoon, its commander heaving a great sigh of relief, marched back to the billets.

Eric Collier returned from leave at the end of the week. At the first possible opportunity, the junior subaltern confronted him, only to find that his friend passionately and emphatically denied any knowledge of the hoax. He had certainly not taken part in any such performance, nor had he heard anything about it. He had had much better things to do with his time during his precious leave. Must have been someone else – but a good show, all the same!

Still not entirely convinced, the junior subaltern, in Holt a few days later to collect company pay from the bank, took the chance to seek out Ben in his usual mid-day haunt at the bar of The Feathers. The taxi-driver assured him that the French officers whom he had collected at Sheringham station were indeed what they purported to be: members of the Free French forces. He had delivered them to their new HQ at Kelling Street. On his return journey, the junior subaltern made a slight detour. Sure enough, as Ben had said, Kelling Pines had been taken over by the French; there was a sentry on the gate, and the Free French flag flew over the front door. He returned to Sheringham greatly relieved that he had resisted the temptation to pull that beautiful, pointed beard.

Early in 1940, the battalion, then guarding the coastline around Blakeney, was inspected by a very high-ranking VIP. A formal parade was required, with only those on essential duties excused. On the appointed day The Royal Scots Fusiliers were drawn up on the makeshift parade ground outside the Blakeney Hotel, the battalion HQ. The weather was unkind: cold, driving sleet and a piercing wind. So vile were the conditions that Sally and Jock, the dogs owned by the CO and the second-in command respectively, which usually kept close to the heels of their masters on any parade, wisely remained in the shelter of the hotel porch from which they could watch the proceedings in relative and enviable comfort. Half an hour passed: no sign of the VIP. The troops were now soaked to the skin, blanco dripping from equipment and gaiters. The dogs had long since wisely retired to a more comfortable position within the hotel. At long last the convoy arrived. The personage, well protected against the elements, walked briskly through the ranks of the battalion, stopping not once to speak personally to any of the men who had waited for nearly an hour in such miserable conditions. Then, after a brief word with the CO, he returned to his comfortable limousine. No greeting of any kind, no short speech, no explanation or apology for having kept the troops waiting. As the cars drove away, the three cheers called by Colonel Syfret were certainly less than earshattering.

Very different also was another occasion which took place when B Company was detailed to form part of the guard protecting the royal family at Sandringham over the Christmas and New Year period. The junior subaltern was acting company commander in the absence of Captain Smith, hors-de-combat following his car accident in Sheringham. One morning a message was received from the estate office. The King would be pleased to meet later that day over refreshments all those who could be spared from the protection duties.

The junior subaltern liaised with his opposite number in The Welch Regiment; it was agreed that each could spare two officers and 20 men. Word to that effect was sent to the Sandringham office.

When they arrived at the house, the RSF party was led through a side entrance into a spacious room on the ground floor. It had been cleared of furniture, apart from a long oak table placed against one wall. Large portraits of British and European dignitaries of past years looked down from below an ornate ceiling from the centre of which hung a large chandelier.

Having been joined by the Welch party, they were welcomed by an RN lieutenant-commander, who then spoke briefly to them. He explained that the King did not want undue ceremony, but wished only to thank them for their services, and to show his gratitude and appreciation. Refreshments would be offered: sandwiches, scones, cakes, biscuits: beer for the men, sherry for the officers. They would NOT help themselves! If addressed personally, they would call the King 'Sir' and the Queen, if she was present, 'Ma'am'. He would indicate when the time had come to take their leave.

Their briefing had just finished when the double doors at the far end of the room opened, and King George entered, dressed informally in tweeds. The naval officer introduced the army officers, to each of whom the King said a few words of thanks. He then addressed the men generally, apologising for "spoiling their Christmas", and explaining that by their presence at Sandringham they had enabled him and his family to enjoy a short holiday which would not have been possible without their being there to protect them. For this, he was very grateful. When he had finished speaking, the doors opened again; maids and footmen entered, carrying trays of food and drink, to move amongst the guests with these refreshments. The King, now joined by Queen Elizabeth, spoke a few words individually to every single man. It appeared to the junior subaltern that this did not come easily to him; he seemed essentially to be a shy person, and the occasion involved real effort on his part.

The Queen was much easier in her manner, and helped the men to relax as well. From time to time she brought a gust of laughter from the little groups which tended to collect around her. She seemed genuinely interested when she heard that the junior subaltern had been a boarder at Loretto School, quite close to the house where she had often stayed as a child, and at which several of her cousins had been pupils. She remembered, too, the occasion in 1935, when Loretto had provided part of the guard of honour for the General Assembly at Holyrood at a time when the King and she, then Duke and Duchess of York, had been attending that function. They had both been amused to read the report in the press that 'the Loretto boys looked very pretty in their bright red and white dresses.'

After about half an hour or so, the naval officer indicated discreetly to the junior subaltern that it was time to go. He and the Welch company commander approached the King to take their leave. That done, the guests were ushered out into the main hall, whereupon the two groups returned to their respective camps in the woods.

The effect on the troops was obvious. Many – probably most – had never seen the King in whose name they were supposedly fighting, except perhaps briefly on a cinema screen. Yet that afternoon he had spoken to each one personally. Royalty was no longer abstract and remote: it was tangible. It could speak to them; it could dispose cakes and ale. As they marched back to camp their pride could almost be felt. As one fusilier was heard to remark, no doubt with a previous VIP occasion in mind, "Theys yins (meaning the King and Queen) widnay hae left us stanning in the rain for oors – he's a real gent, and she's a gey guid wee lassie!" Coming as it did from a staunch peacetime member of the Cowcaddens branch of the Communist Party, this observation was praise indeed.

19. BLACKER BOMBARD

After the retreat from Dunkirk, the British army was desperately short of weaponry and armour, so much having been abandoned in France. The battalions which had been rushed to defend the south and east coasts of England, the most likely targets of the expected and imminent German invasion, had presumably been given the best available; but even this was woefully and pathetically insufficient and inadequate.

The RSF were no exception. Each company had less than one third of its essential establishment in arms and in transport, some of the latter still being composed of the civilian vehicles which had been requisitioned earlier in Melton Mowbray. The thought of 11 Platoon grinding into action against the might of the German army, carried in their converted Co-op van, might have been hilarious had it not been so tragically pathetic. Arrangements had also been made with the local 'bus company for the hiring of their vehicles in any emergency. The junior subaltern conjured up the vision of hurrying to the 'phone box, asking the exchange for Holt 227, and ordering a char-a-banc to be sent round to take his platoon to the scene of battle, provided, of course, that a driver were available. The reality was that there was only one truck, a Bedford 30 hundredweight, for the whole of B Company, instead of the five that were on the official establishment: this in addition to the company commander's Hillman PU. Weapons were totally inadequate. Each man had his own rifle, a 1914-18 Lee-Enfield. The platoon had one Bren light machine gun instead of three, one 2-inch mortar instead of three; ammunition was so limited that practice with live rounds was severely restricted. Each manned defensive position had one Boer War Hotchkiss machine gun, belt-fed. It was not until all threat of invasion was thought to be past that the latter could be tested, when most were found to be useless: much of the ammunition was of an incorrect calibre.

Each platoon was expected to maintain its own supply of petrol bombs, made by themselves. These, commonly known as Molotov cocktails, were crude weapons, easily assembled. An old beer or lemonade bottle was filled with a mixture of petrol and oil; its neck was stuffed with a piece of rag which acted as a fuse. To this was attached an ignition fuzee. The bomb was to be flung at the enemy invaders or, according to the brigadier, dropped down the turret of an enemy tank. Presumably, thought the junior subaltern, the said enemy tank would stop in a convenient place and its commander would politely open the turret hatch to allow the entry of the flaming missile.

These Molotov cocktails were liable to spontaneous combustion, so had to be packed in beer or milk crates and kept where they could not damage their own side. Usually a small pit was dug into which the crate was put, and given protection against the weather. As these weapons were unofficial, and appeared on no inventory, they tended to become forgotten because of the frequent change-over of units. In time, nature took over and concealed them. Two years after the end of the war, the former junior subaltern, returning on a nostalgic visit, found two of his crates; one in the roadside ditch at Oak Wood, near Weybourne, one in a heather-covered hole by the crossroads at Pretty Corner in Upper Sheringham. Both crates were intact, each with its 24 bottles complete. He toyed with the idea of setting the whole lot alight in joyful celebration, but resisted the temptation. They would have made a glorious blaze, but the occupants of Sheringham Hall and other residents nearby might not have been so appreciative. Instead, as a dutiful citizen, he informed the authorities. His cache of Molotovs on Beeston Hump had disappeared along with its crate, probably over the cliff, as considerable erosion had taken place. There are no doubt many other crates of cocktails distributed in hidden and long-forgotten little holes all along the north Norfolk coast.

Several other ideas were proposed which came to naught. Suggestions were made that the sea could be set alight by anchoring large drums of petrol below low water mark, these to be activated when the invaders neared the shore. Experiments had been made, it was said, on the south coast, but the scheme had been abandoned; apparently it was effective only when the sea was very calm. In the banks of some of the lanes which led from the beach through to gaps on the north Norfolk coast, at East and West Runton, Weybourne and elsewhere, barrels of petrol and oil had been placed, these to be exploded by certain men detailed for the unenviable task. Many soldiers doubted the effectiveness of this and other similar measures. The use of well-tried and existing equipment would be preferable: mines laid, for instance, on the approach roads. But this of course would interfere with the passage of what civilian traffic remained. There was still a great reluctance, perhaps not surprisingly, on the part of the local inhabitants to regard the coast as the real front line of battle, as it then undoubtedly was; whilst the army was constantly being urged to refrain from upsetting the civilians.

Strange weapons would suddenly be issued, discovered no doubt in long-forgotten stores, or the latest product of some boffin's imagination. Most were more trouble than they were worth, and were quickly abandoned. One day in the late summer of 1940, alongside the useless revolving turret and future tadpole sanctuary beside Oak Wood a strange device, going by the name of Blacker Bombard, was erected. An officer of the Royal Artillery came to demonstrate this new and hitherto secret weapon to the men of 11 Platoon. After much preliminary fiddling, and the consulting of manuals, all was pronounced ready. The men were invited to imagine that a solitary tree some 300 yards away was an advancing enemy tank. 11 Platoon's collective mental processes were not very great, but they did their combined best. The officer inserted the missile, which resembled a short, squat mortar bomb, then made some slight adjustments. By this time, the junior subaltern silently decided, the imaginary tank would no longer be 300 yards away, but in amongst them. No matter.

The demonstration officer, satisfied that the weapon was now all ready, pulled sharply on a cord, just as if he were starting up a reluctant motor mower; whereupon the obese projectile hopped out of the Bombard, described a slow and lazy parabola, and flopped wearily into the standing corn at the edge of the field across the road, some 20 yards away. The men of 11 Platoon, who had been watching the demonstration with less than rapt attention, were suddenly galvanised into life, and beat their platoon commander by a short head in their dash to the protection of the nearby slit trenches, the gunner officer coming a poor third. The expected explosion however did not materialise. 11 Platoon, suspicious as always of the actions of officers, remained firmly trench-bound whilst the gunner captain made a cautious reconnaissance before pronouncing all was safe.

Nevertheless, he said, the bomb should on no account be touched; sappers would deal with it later. He sent his driver to collect some warning flags and poles from nearby Weybourne Camp; these were placed in a circle of about 50 yards radius around the dormant projectile, their red tops fluttering just above the corn. He asked that a sentry be posted until the arrival of the Royal Engineers, to discourage any curious nosey-parkers, and departed to make the necessary arrangements.

11 Platoon, required for other duties, were extracted from their refuge with some reluctance, and marched off towards Sheringham. leaving behind Fusilier O'Hara to guard the danger area, the latter having been detailed for his task by Sergeant Canning. Odd jobs such as this were often given to O'Hara. Anyone less fitted to be a soldier would be hard to find; as his companions said, he was a general disaster area. When he tried to march, left arm would swing with left leg, right arm with right leg. When anything remotely resembling a ceremonial parade was ordered O'Hara was carefully hidden away, or was reported sick. On the ranges during initial training he had hit almost everything, including very nearly the company sergeant-major, except the target. He seldom had all his own regulation kit or equipment; this did not bother him too much, for he 'borrowed' readily from his fellow soldiers without troubling to ask their permission.

On one memorable occasion, on being asked his name by a visiting VIP, he replied, "Jimmy O'Hara, what's yours, mate?" He was transferred to HQ Company for a while, it being thought that he might be of some use in general fatigue duties; but after he had managed to put a bucket of potato peelings to boil on the stove and the peeled spuds into the swill bin, and had later emptied an entire bag of salt into the stew, the cooks protested so strongly that he was hastily returned to B Company and 11 Platoon. O'Hara always insisted that he was in the army by mistake. As an Irishman living in Glasgow he claimed he should have been exempt, but somehow he had been caught up in the system. He voiced a garbled and complicated story concerning a fracas in the Jubilee Bar in Maryhill Road which had led to his being enlisted. Because of his many deficiencies, he was usually the one detailed by his platoon sergeant for any odd jobs that arose where it would be difficult even for O'Hara to put his foot in it. But, as he marched off with his men, the junior subaltern, observing who was standing guard on the errant missile, hoped that his sergeant had not made a serious error of judgement.

That afternoon, working on defences beside the railway line, he received an urgent summons to return to Oak Wood. There he found the demonstration officer with a few sappers, their truck, and several curious spectators. A sulky-looking O'Hara stood nearby, a Woodbine dangling from his lip, his rifle propped against a tree. The general scene had changed considerably since the morning, for harvesting had begun, and already that section of the field into which the bomb had fallen, and which had been marked off with flags, had been reduced to stubble. Of the flagpoles, and of the missile itself, there was no sign. The anxious RA officer indicated that he had been unable to extract much sense from O'Hara. The junior subaltern, with a more intimate understanding of that soldier's mental processes, and a greater knowledge of the severe limitations of his vocabulary, asked him what had happened. The gist of the ensuing explanations, omitting the copious use of certain expletives which O'Hara employed impartially as noun, verb, adverb or adjective, not aggressively but as a matter of syntax, was that this civvy bloke had come along and asked rudely what he – O'Hara – thought he was doing there, and why these flag poles had been stuck in his field; and would he remove them pronto as the corn was about to be cut; and if O'Hara was going to play soldiers, would he please go and do that elsewhere. O'Hara gave the distinct impression that 'the bloke' had not been exactly polite; he had taken strong umbrage to the verbal assault and had retired in high dudgeon to the slit trench to have a smoke, only to be chivvied again by the returned demonstration officer. He had no idea where the flag poles, nor, more importantly, the bomb had gone, and implied that he couldn't care less.

The two officers hurried across the field to the place where the farmer was now working, to try and find out more, and to receive the latter's version of what had happened. This corresponded quite closely to what O'Hara had said, though expressed in somewhat different language. The farmer told them clearly that he was not going to have his harvest delayed by any pretty flags stuck up without permission in his field. As these were on his property, he had removed them; they now belonged to him. They would come in handy next year as stakes for his wife's runner beans.

He was asked about the bomb. "What bomb?" The demonstration officer, now even more anxious looking, explained. "Oh, that's what that thing was!" Apparently the dog – "silly useless bitch" – had carried it back to the farmhouse – "thinks she's a bloody retriever" – and deposited it proudly on the kitchen floor. His wife had picked it up and put it in the bin with the other rubbish. The demonstration officer, growing paler by the second, asked if it were still there. The farmer replied that one of his 'dizzy, flighty no-use land girls" had been told to dump the lot over the cliff and into the sea: "no damn council dust-cart these days". Tide was now well on the ebb, so it would all have gone. A quick visit to the cliff top confirmed this; a heavy sea was running, with a strong under-tow. No sign on the beach of any rubbish – nor Bombard missile. The farmer, quite unrepentant, shrugged off the warning about the danger of handling strange objects and returned to his harvesting, no doubt further to berate his unfortunate female assistants. The two officers somewhat subdued, returned to Oak Wood.

The junior subaltern did not envy his companion his task of explaining the day's activities to his superiors; but that was not his problem, for which he was indeed thankful. Nothing more was heard of the Blacker Bombard, much to the relief of 11 Platoon. It might well be maintained that Fusilier O'Hara had at last made his own small contribution to the general war effort, if only in a negative way.

20. SALTHOUSE ROULETTE

Salthouse in the depths of winter was not exactly one of the troops' favourite places. Their off-duty billets were small and cramped. The defence posts were separated from the village itself by salt marshes which were often whipped day and night by a fierce wind which carried with it snow, sleet or rain, and sometimes hail stones sharp enough to cut exposed flesh; balaclava helmets were necessities rather than luxuries, but were nevertheless banned by order of the brigadier, who didn't believe in mollycoddling his men. The villagers were kind and hospitable, but entertainment was very limited. The one small pub was frequently devoid of stock. When supplies were delivered, the beer was, not surprisingly, reserved for the regular customers. There was still much to be done to improve the defences, and wrestling with lengths of tubular scaffolding and barbed wire, whilst being battered by wind and soaked by driving rain, was an occupation that could appeal to none but a confirmed masochist. Setting up tank traps or laying mines could be equally unpleasant. On two nights out of every three the men were on duty, manning the beach positions or patrolling the marshes. B Company seemed to have more than their fair share of the Salthouse detail, and 11 Platoon considered that, as usual, they had more of their fair share of unpleasant jobs.

There were two brighter spots to brighten the gloom, both concerned the inner man; and did not Napoleon once remark that an army marched upon its stomach? Near the centre of the village, at the rear of one of the flint-walled cottages, was a small bakery. Every day without fail, the owners of this bakery produced a large batch of fresh muffins. Where they obtained their supplies, or the golden syrup to go with the muffins, nobody knew or cared. From about 8 am every morning the glorious aroma of baking began to pervade the entire village. It reached the nostrils of the fusiliers working on the scaffolding; it roused the taste buds of the men digging the anti-tank trap between the main road and the marshes; it hastened the footsteps of the sections returning from night duty at Rocket House. The daily expectation, the thought of the warm, soft muffin, the sweet trickle of syrup, was almost, but not quite, as good as the ultimate reality. At 11 am – 1100 hrs, as the army insisted – the whistle would blow to begin the 15-minute break and all B Company, sentries excepted, would descend on the source of the aroma, there to form an orderly queue, two pence in hand, for that was all that was charged. That little baker did more for the morale of B Company than the mouthings of any politicians, and certainly a great deal more than the perfunctory visits of VIPs.

On two days each week, the delicious offerings of the bake house were supplemented by the arrival of the WRI van, manned by two large, jolly and resourceful ladies who dispensed with rapid efficiency mugs of steaming, sweet tea at the price of one penny per mug, with a 'wad' (a slab of fruit cake) a penny extra. Their arrival was timed to coincide with the 11 am break, and the distribution of muffins, so it was possible for a fusilier, if he were in funds, to do himself proud on a hot muffin, a wad, and a mug of tea, all for the sum of only fourpence.

Higher authority, in the person of the brigadier, was apt to arrive on a tour of inspection at about this hour. The 11 o'clock break was supposed to last for 10 minutes only. This gave insufficient time for men working at the far end of the village to enjoy their refreshment, so Captain Smith had added an unofficial five minutes. This concession more than paid its way by the enhancement of morale: to have kept strictly to the 10-minute order would have resulted in extreme bloody-mindedness. But 'authority' would not have acknowledged this, so to avoid trouble, officers or NCOs were placed in strategic positions to give warning of any approach of official cars by agreed signals, on the receipt of which everyone would scurry back to work until all was clear again.

One day the junior subaltern had just collected his hot muffin, syrup gently oozing from its warm perimeter, when he heard the alarm signals. He was determined not to be deprived of his little luxury on a day when wind and rain were relentless in their ferocity. As he ran to join his platoon on the village green, he wrapped his steaming muffin in a handkerchief and stuffed the resulting parcel into the inside pocket of his battledress blouse, where it immediately began to act as a hot water bottle.

The brigadier's car drew up beside the scaffolding upon which his men were working. "He would choose us today," muttered the junior subaltern to himself. The fusiliers, having had time to wolf down their own muffins, were giving a good impression of industry – a quality not normally associated with 11 Platoon – but the brigadier seemed reluctant to move on. He had several questions to put to the platoon commander about the defences. As he replied, the latter began to feel the syrup, warmed by its enclosing muffin, and no doubt by bodily heat, gently dripping down his chest inside his shirt. By the time the brigadier had finished his questions, had made some rather futile suggestions and had departed, no doubt to the comfort of a warm mess at Kelling, the syrup had reached his waistline, and seemed to be congealing. Handing over his command to Sergeant Canning, he retired to the nearby telephone box, where he took off his blouse to inspect the damage. It was not a pretty sight. All that remained of his beautiful muffin was a yellow, soggy mess, rapidly congealing inside his blouse, down the front of his shirt and around his waist. All warmth had gone. As he replaced his battledress top, he reflected sadly that he would not be able to change until work ended at dusk and he could withdraw to his billet.

Almost all flint-walled, the cottages and small houses of the village were strung along the landward side of the coast road, with some others clustered around the village green. On the hillside above, old, beautiful and dominating, stood the church, in the vaults of which, it was said, smugglers in the distant – and indeed, according to local gossip, the not-so-distant – past had stored their cargoes. A tunnel was believed to run from the church to a spot near the village inn, though its exact whereabouts was unknown.

Sitting ugly and incongruous between church above and flint village below had recently been built a cluster of red-brick houses. One of these had been requisitioned for use as B Company officers' mess. On the ground floor were rooms used for dining and sitting; on the first floor, around a small landing were three bedrooms and a bathroom. It was to one of these bedrooms that the junior subaltern retired to change into clean and dry uniform. The incessant rain had converted the syrup muffin mixture into something unbelievably horrid and sticky; he could just imagine the remarks which his batman, Percival, would conjure up when he collected the clothes for washing.

He was the first in the billet, so for once the bathroom was free – and the water was hot! He filled the bath to a point well above the line which denoted the permitted limit: a sort of bathing plimsoll line. The others would complain about the lack of hot water when they came in – but let them! He deserved his little luxury after the day he had suffered. He relaxed in the glorious, steamy, soapy warmth. As he lay there, he could see the neat, round hole drilled in the bathroom door, plugged effectively if not inconspicuously with some soap; and he recalled with some amusement its origin.

One evening he and a fellow officer, Pete Rayner, commander of 10 Platoon, found themselves alone in the mess. The other two subalterns were on duty in the marshes; Captain Smith, observing pointedly that for once the others had left some hot water, had departed upstairs to have a bath and an early night. The junior subaltern was quite content to sit and read, enjoying his armchair and the comfort of a warm fire, listening to the hail battering on the window, glad to be off duty. But Pete was a restless soul, always looking for something to do. He was for ever thinking out new ways of amusing himself. His latest was an adaptation of Russian Roulette, substituting blank bullets for live rounds, and making it into a betting game. Pete was a keen gambler, ready to put his money on almost anything; it pained him that his impecunious fellow officers seldom took up the challenges which he threw down. Eventually, in response to his repeated badgering, the junior subaltern reluctantly put away his book, and the two of them made their way upstairs to the bedroom which they shared. Captain Smith had insisted that this game should not be played in the general mess room. In fact, he disapproved of the whole idea, and only grudgingly agreed to its being played when Pete amended the rules. A target, usually some picture taken from an old magazine, was now used, and proper revolver procedures, with aiming points called for every 'shot', were correctly followed. Thus Pete's game might be said to have some remote military value.

Whilst the latter produced his Smith and Wesson 38 revolver, and filled one of the six chambers with a blank cartridge from the box which he kept in his chest of drawers, the junior subaltern pinned the target to the bedroom door: a detailed picture of Trafalgar Square, torn from the Illustrated London News. As he did so, he was glad to hear the voice of Captain Smith singing in his bath, loudly, cheerfully and tunelessly as was his wont. The comparatively subdued 'crack' of a blank cartridge exploding should not disturb him.

In turns, each officer rotated the revolver chamber, named his target, aimed, and pressed the trigger. "Nelson, 4 o'clock 'bus, O for Ovaltine, aim, fire": a gentle 'click'. The 5 to 1 chance of the round being in the chamber was, as always, remote. Pete's fourth or fifth turn came. "Policeman, 12 o'clock, Belisha beacon, aim, fire". Not this time the gentle ‘click’, but the loud ‘crack’ of a live round being fired. “Daisy, Daisy, give me…” emanating from the bathroom ended abruptly in a loud yell. Before the two officers had time to recover from their surprised shock, the door was flung open, and an irate, towel-clad steaming company commander stood there, drippingly demanding an explanation. “Damned nearly killed me, you b- idiots,” he raged. He grabbed the revolver from the table, broke it to check it was unloaded, picked up the ejected cartridge case, and stamped off back to the bathroom, words such as “court martial”, “should be cashiered” echoing above the damp footprints on the landing floor.

Pete, having absorbed the ensuing storm of abuse from the junior subaltern, took up the box of supposedly blank cartridges, and emptied its contents on to the bed. All had the coloured dot which denoted that they were blanks, not live. He assured his friend that he had checked carefully the round before inserting it in the revolver: and Pete, whatever his other faults, was a good and reliable military man. But live bullet it certainly had been. There was a neat, round hole pierced in the door panel behind the target nominated by the firer: Pete’s aim had certainly been good.

They heard Captain Smith leave the bathroom and retire to his bedroom. The coast was now clear. They decided to find out where the bullet had ended up. Directly opposite their bedroom door was the bathroom, in the door of which a similar neat hole had been drilled. They entered the bathroom. On the opposite wall, a couple of feet above the bath, they could see a hole in the plaster which had not been there before: long cracks led out from it like ripples in a pool of water. No wonder Captain Smith had been so annoyed: no wonder that ‘Daisy, Daisy’ had come to such an abrupt conclusion: the bullet must have passed only a few inches above the company commander’s head. Peter produced a penknife and gently prized the spent bullet from its plastery resting place.

Next morning, the two officers were summoned to the company office, where Captain Smith said just what he thought of them in no uncertain terms. But no court martial. He picked up the used cartridge case which lay on his desk, and showed it to them. It held the mark which designated it as a blank, not a live, cartridge: a manufacturer’s mistake. The interview ended with the company commander’s strict instructions that the remaining rounds were to be destroyed and that Russian Roulette was forthwith prohibited. As the two relieved officers saluted and quit the office, Pete grinned and said to his companion:

"Don't forget: I won last night, you owe me five bob!"

As the junior subaltern turned on the hot once again to replenish his bath, his fingers touched the hole in the plaster. Captain Smith certainly did have a narrow shave. Good thing he hadn't been sitting up at the time. He lay back again, luxuriating in the warm water, and idly wondered just what the house owners would make of these three strange holes when they returned to their home after the war. Three small holes in the bedroom door, in the bathroom door, in the bathroom wall. Three neat, round holes all in a nice, straight military line. What indeed would they make of that?

His idle musings were interrupted by the sound of heavy footsteps on the uncarpeted stairs. Captain Smith had returned. He sighed: he'd better get out. Reluctantly, he hooked a foot behind the chain, and gently removed the bathplug.

21. CLOAK AND DAGGER

Throughout the war, and especially during the earlier years, the people of Britain were constantly being exhorted to be vigilant. Posters drawn by Fougasse bearing the message 'Walls Have Ears' or 'Careless Talk Costs Lives', everywhere reminded them that spies might be in their midst. Newspapers carried stories of how German agents had operated behind Allied lines in France, dropped by parachute, disguised as nuns or nurses; lurid tales of espionage were rife. Exaggerated these undoubtedly were; but the danger was very real, and very obvious to the troops whose task it was to guard the Norfolk coast. A glance at the map was sufficient to show that between Hunstanton and Great Yarmouth there were many places where a resourceful enemy agent might safely land unseen and unchallenged. The few battalions were too thin on the ground, too widely extended, to be able to keep the entire coastline under observation. Defensive posts at especially vulnerable sectors were manned; behind them constant and vigorous night patrols were active; but any enemy spy, determined and alert, would be unlikely and unfortunate to be intercepted.

By now, The Royal Scots Fusiliers were at last approaching full strength, and the post of intelligence officer could be established. Wee Steevie, scenting a cushy job amongst the commanding officer's entourage, landed the position. He moved into the HQ mess with obvious pleasure. No orderly officer duties; a comfortable bedroom; no further unpleasant nights on patrol in the Salthouse marshes, or on watch on Weybourne Hope. An enviable job at that time; less enviable later in the war when the IO was often required to navigate the battalion during any approach march into battle.

Steevie was not one to minimise the importance of his new position, and took every opportunity to exalt his self-esteem. Even his penchant for mischievous practical jokes was diminished; he no longer had time for such frivolities. Orders and advice were issued in abundance.

Frequent spot checks were made on company and platoon positions. His former popularity amongst his fellow officers waned considerably; although still of junior rank, he represented the commanding officer, and the company commander whom he censured for supposed deficiencies in anti-espionage measures had to accept his criticisms, however reluctantly. He summoned officers and NCOs to HQ to listen to lectures given by Captain Gordon Gilmot, who had served with the 1st Battalion in France before Dunkirk. The latter was an accomplished jazz pianist who had quickly established a local reputation as an entertainer on the piano in the bar lounge of the Dormy Hotel; his rendering of 'The Waiter and the Porter and the Upstairs Maid' was one never to be forgotten by those fortunate enough to hear it.

One day, when B Company were stationed at East Runton, a message was received ordering Lieutenant Collier and the junior subaltern to report at once to battalion HQ in Sheringham. There, they were told that the intelligence officer wanted to see them. Wee Steevie acknowledged their somewhat exaggerated salutes (all three officers were of equal seniority), and asked them to sit down. He had a matter of importance to discuss, top secret. Eric Collier at once put his finger to his lips, rose from his chair, tip-toed over to the door, then flung it suddenly wide open, much to the astonishment of the company quartermaster sergeant and the company clerk in the adjoining room. Closing the door, Eric resumed his seat. "Just checking, Steevie," he said, "can't be too careful. Walls have ears and all that, you know!" How he managed to keep a straight face, the junior subaltern will never understand.

Apparently undisturbed by this demonstration of dramatic security, the IO explained why he had required their presence. He had received reports of the suspicious activities of two visitors in West Runton: two young women who seemed to be going out of their way to befriend various officers in the RA and other units. They were often to be seen near defence positions. The Military Police had checked their restricted-area permits which appeared to be in order; but he, Steevie, was not satisfied. He wanted Collier and the junior subaltern to make their acquaintance, find out all they could, and report back to him. The two girls usually went to the Saturday evening dances at the Village Inn in West Runton; that would provide a good opportunity to begin the surveillance operation.

The IO brushed aside the junior subaltern's objection that he would be on patrol duty on Saturday evening. Orders could be given to free him. His mind boggled at the thought of his company commander's reactions to the order that two of his officers should be taken off patrol duties in order to attend a village dance, but refrained from comment. Wee Steevie ended the conference by stating a time when he would meet them on the coming Saturday to point out the two suspects.

As expected, Captain Smith, received the order with less than delight, but there was nothing he could do about it, except to glower at his two junior officers when, attired in full service dress, they set out to meet Wee Steevie at the bar of the Village Inn in West Runton. The dance was in full swing by the time they arrived – because of war-time restrictions it always began early and ended at 10.30 pm – and the place was packed. Steevie finished off his pint and gladly accepted another one. "They're here," he said, "come, and I'll point them out." The three men, glasses in hand, made their way across the room to the door which led directly into the dance hall. The immediate impression was of a dull khaki swirl of humanity within an orbit of hazy tobacco smoke, responding energetically to an enthusiastic, if rather inexpert, dance band. Nearly all those on the dance floor were RA and ATS, men and women from Weybourne camp, with a smattering of RAF blue. The few civilian dancers were therefore conspicuous, none more so than the two girls whom Steevie indicated.

Their summer frocks stood out delightfully cool and bright as the closely-packed throng circled the floor. "Got them?" asked Wee Steevie. The two officers nodded. "I'll be off then, " said the IO, draining his glass; "don't want them to see me. Report first thing tomorrow."

The moment he had gone, Eric exploded in a gust of laughter, to the surprise of his companion who had been expecting some acid comment about Wee Steevie dodging his round (a not uncommon occurrence, for the IO was well-known for the care he took over his pennies). In response to the junior subaltern's look, Eric said, "Another beer, and then I'll tell you the funniest thing you'll have heard in years. Never mind the girls just now – we'll meet them later."

The two men sat on the low wall which surrounded the little garden pond outside the inn, away from the fug, heat and noise of the dance hall, enjoying the cool of the evening, sipping their ale. Eric explained. He had often met the girls before the war. Their names were Lynette and Betty and they were nieces of the brigadier who had for many years now owned a house in West Runton which he had used pre-war as a holiday home. Recently he had allowed his two nieces, who worked with the American Ambulance in Nottingham, to stay in the house when on leave. Their restricted-area passes were perfectly genuine. They were certainly no spies.

"Well, that's that," said the junior subaltern, "we'll just have to tell Wee Steevie in the morning." Eric thought for a moment, then replied, "That would be a pity; he'll be so disappointed not to hit the headlines as a big, spy-catching hero! Hold your horses, I'll be back in a jiffy." So saying, he disappeared into the inn, to return in a few minutes accompanied by the two girls and carrying a tray of drinks which he deposited on a nearby bench before making the necessary introductions. The four sat chatting and drinking beside the little pond. The strains of 'Goodnight sweetheart', the signing-off tune of the RAF band, vibrated on the cool night air. "Drink up," said Eric to the junior subaltern, "we are going to the girls' house for coffee. I'll take the glasses back, then catch you up."

The house was only a short distance away, up a quiet side street in the village. The girls led the way into a large, comfortable sitting room, adjusted the black-out curtains, switched on the lights and departed to the kitchen. During their absence, Eric explained his idea. He would report to Wee Steevie that the two girls were quite all right, no security risk whatever, and that the IO had nothing to worry about. This would cover themselves. But he would not tell him that the girls were related to the brigadier. Starting the next day, the girls would try to behave in a very suspicious manner, preferably in places and at times when they might be observed by the IO himself. They would hang around HQ, be seen talking to soldiers close to defence posts, ask apparently leading questions, go out for picnics on the cliff tops, and so on. That would keep Steevie happy, whilst Eric and the junior subaltern, having reported that the girls were no security threat, could not be blamed if, or when, the IO learnt the truth.

Lynette and Betty, having returned with coffee, entered into the plan with enthusiasm. They had been finding life a trifle boring being unable, because of war restrictions, to enjoy the normal activities associated with a seaside holiday. Eric suggested various situations which might be exploited, and the girls themselves came forward with other ideas. The junior subaltern even began to feel a twinge of pity for the IO.

Next morning, Eric reported to Wee Steevie as arranged. The following few days were exceptionally busy, and the junior subaltern had no chance to wonder about the progress of the plan; but on Thursday evening Wee Steevie came through on the field telephone. "Were they sure the girls were O.K?" The IO himself had seen them behave very furtively. The junior subaltern repeated his opinion that there was no security risk. Wee Steevie strongly disagreed. If that was his opinion, then it was no use asking him and Eric to make further enquiries. He – the IO – would have to take personal action. "Why have I always to do everything myself?" he complained. Eric later received the news with delight. The girls must be doing their job well.

A few days later, visiting Battalion HQ, he took the chance to call in to see the IO, to be told that the latter had opened a file on the activities of the suspects. When Eric again emphasised that no evidence had been found to doubt the two girls, and that they were just innocent holiday-makers with genuine passes, and suggested that the IO should drop the whole matter, Wee Steevie became (as Eric had expected and hoped) even more stubborn and determined. He made it plain that he didn't think much of their conclusions. Once his own investigations were complete, he fully intended to send the file to Brigade HQ, with his recommendations. That evening Eric and the junior subaltern spent a happy, if perhaps spiteful, half-hour wondering just what the brigadier's reactions would be to the allegations that his favourite nieces were possible spies. He was justifiably renowned for his fiery temper.

Nothing more was heard of the matter for several days. Lynette and Betty, their holiday over, had returned to Nottingham, and neither Eric nor the junior subaltern had any cause to visit HQ, until at the end of the month, the former was sent into Sheringham by his company commander to meet a newly-joined officer, whom he was to take to Battalion HQ to meet the CO, before bringing him out to B Company. Whilst the new arrival was in the CO's office, Eric sought out Wee Steevie, but was given a very cool reception. In reply to his innocent enquiry as to how the spy investigation was proceeding, the IO showed great reluctance to discuss the matter; the case was out of his hands. The girls, having left the area, were no longer his responsibility. When Eric reminded him that he and the junior subaltern had reported nothing amiss, Wee Steevie gave him a hard and suspicious look, but said no more.

Fellow officers noticed that he had recently been much subdued, without his customary bumptiousness. Rumour had it that he had received an almighty rocket from the brigadier about something, but the reason was not known. Company commanders were pleased that the previous string of irritating orders on security had suddenly been cut short. Gradually the whole incident faded into obscurity. From time to time, Eric and the junior subaltern recalled it with pleasure. They knew, however, that Wee Steevie must have had his own suspicions that he had been 'set-up', although he never alluded to the matter; and the IO had a long memory. B Company moved to the Holkham area, without much contact with Battalion HQ. Eric himself was shortly afterwards successful in his application to join the RAF, and left the battalion.

Some weeks later the junior subaltern was granted his precious leave, long overdue, which he spent at his parents' home in Glasgow. Whilst there, he received a 'phone call from Les Rowell, the assistant adjutant, to tell him that a mutual friend of theirs, Jackie Robertson, had been posted to one of the new commando units; there would be a tremendous party to send him off; could he – the junior subaltern – come back from leave a day early, otherwise he would miss the great occasion?

The rail journey from Glasgow to Sheringham during war-time was never easy. It involved changes of trains at Edinburgh, Peterborough and Melton Constable. It was a tedious journey; no sleepers available, no refreshment facilities except at stations. On this occasion, because of enemy air action, there were diversions, and he found himself unexpectedly deposited on a platform in Rugby, with the information that a connection to Peterborough would depart in three hours' time. It was a pleasant morning, so he decided to explore the town rather than hang around the station.

After a stroll along some of the main streets, where traffic was light and he had a chance to stop and gaze at the more interesting buildings, he decided he should find out how to reach Rugby School, at which some of his friends had been pupils. This was less easy than he had hoped; most of those of whom he asked directions were themselves strangers to the town. Earlier he had passed a post office, so he decided to retrace his steps and enquire there; he had almost reached it when he was stopped by two men, one of whom politely asked him his name. Somewhat surprised, the junior subaltern asked the reason for the request. The man produced a small wallet, in which was a card showing the holder to be a member of British Intelligence. He thereupon gave his name, only to be asked what he was doing in Rugby. He explained. The men, apparently unimpressed by his reply, politely but firmly insisted that he accompany them to their office in a nearby building.

There they told him that they had been following him for some time, noting his unusual interest in various buildings of importance in the town. He again explained the circumstances. The men asked further questions, then requested his leave pass and identity discs. The fact that his pass did not expire for another 36 hours did not escape their attention. Why was he returning so early? Most people left their return until the last possible minute. Even to his own ears, the junior subaltern's explanation seemed feeble. The two men left the room, saying they would have to check with his unit, and have his statements confirmed; left alone, behind a locked door, virtually a prisoner, he took stock. He didn't feel any great apprehension, just annoyance. Sheringham HQ would confirm his story; but a nuisance, for he would now miss his train connection. However, he had time to spare; it would only mean an even less comfortable journey.

The door opened and the two men returned, but with news which their detainee had certainly not expected. The RSF in Sheringham had indeed confirmed that they had an officer of his name; but the description given just did not fit. Moreover, the officer in question was not expected to return from leave for two more days, nor was there any farewell party planned. The junior subaltern, nonplussed and now very anxious, stuck to his story. He was subjected to a further series of questions, less politely phrased this time, then left alone once more.

He just could not understand it. Ray Buxton, the adjutant, and Les Rowell, the assistant adjutant, were personal friends and could describe him to a T. Moreover, both knew of his proposed early return and the reason for it. Either would have confirmed his story. Suddenly light dawned. He banged loud and long on the locked door until one of his captors appeared. The junior subaltern asked him the position held by the officer to whom he had spoken on the 'phone. "Was it the adjutant or his assistant?" "Neither," was the reply. Both had been unavailable; his call had been put through to the intelligence officer, and it was to the latter that he had spoken. The junior subaltern's suspicions were confirmed. Wee Steevie was having his revenge. He explained – untruthfully – that the IO was new to the RSF and did not know him well (for despite his predicament and annoyance he had no intention of getting his colleague into trouble), then earnestly requested that his Battalion HQ should be contacted once again, and that either the CO himself or the adjutant should be asked the vital questions. The man, obviously impressed by the impassioned and vehement appeal, agreed to do this.

It was not long before both men returned, full of apologies. The adjutant had received the call, and had left them in no doubt at all that the junior subaltern was indeed the person whom he claimed to be. He hoped the latter would understand the need for vigilance and the reasons for his unfortunate detention. As he had now missed the train, a car would be put at his disposal to take him direct to Peterborough, thus avoiding further delay. He must not miss the party!

As the M & GN locomotive huffed and puffed along the last stage of his journey to Sheringham, the junior subaltern wondered what to do about Wee Steevie. His first thoughts had been anything but kindly; but all had been well in the end. The IO could not really be grudged his attempt to gain revenge for the episode of the ‘suspect’ girls. Best perhaps to let bygones be bygones, and call it quits. So quits it would be.

22. WILL YE NO COME BACK AGAIN?

By the summer of 1942, the danger of invasion had declined so much that the coastal defences, scene of so much activity and concern during the previous two years, were now only lightly manned, and patrolling had become minimal. Much more time was being devoted to field training, with units at long last reaching full establishment in weaponry and in transport. At the same time the 11th RSF, along with the other battalions in the brigade, were steadily suffering the loss of many of their experienced young officers, much to the chagrin of their COs. Vacancies thus caused were being filled by newly-commissioned second lieutenants direct from OCTUs. Some of the departing officers were required for service with units fighting overseas, some to strengthen the new and specialist regiments such as the Parachute Regiment and the Commandos. The battalion commanders, try as they would, were powerless to stem this drain on their resources, for these orders were priority ones, and any attempt to circumvent them were fruitless. Of the younger officers who had been with the RSF since the formation of the 11th Battalion at Melton Mowbray, only four now remained: Ray Buxton, who had been made adjutant on Monty's promotion; Les Rowell, assistant adjutant; Wee Steevie, intelligence officer; and the junior subaltern, the only non-specialist amongst them.

He was attending a small arms and explosives course at Sandy, Bedfordshire, when he received orders to return at once to his battalion. On reporting there, he was told that he was to proceed immediately on embarkation leave, during which he would be sent further details. His ultimate destination was unknown, but he was to equip himself with tropical kit. Wally Syfret, the CO, seemed genuinely sorry to lose him: he had approached the brigadier, but to no avail. The 10 days' embarkation leave began instantly, but the CO hoped he would stay with the battalion for one more day; there was to be a special mess night

Will ye no come back again?

to give him a good send-off.

While a lugubrious Percival packed his valise and travelling case, the junior subaltern, having been given the use of the PU, made his round of farewells: Ben at Holt; the Taylors at Beeston; Mrs Smith, the hospitable manageress of the Victoria at Holkham; the Senior Member of the Sheringham Golf Club, the unfortunate victim of his misdirected flour bombs who later had become a good friend, and several others. The mess night was a memorable occasion. Even Monty, the battalion second-in-command and PMC, unbent sufficiently to allow the guest of honour to choose the pipe tunes to be played, a prerogative which hitherto he had reserved strictly for himself; and, what was more, he even expressed approval of the selection made. The party broke up – an appropriate verb – at around 2 am.

Percival's final cup of gunfire tea was even more acceptable than usual when the junior subaltern was awoken in time to catch the 6 am train. Ray was already waiting downstairs; as adjutant as well as friend, he had taken it upon himself to ensure that the departure was properly completed. With baggage safely loaded, the two officers and Percival were driven the short distance to Sheringham station, where the train was already getting up steam. There, the junior subaltern was amazed to see his own 11 Platoon drawn up in smart ranks on the platform, with their original sergeant, now Company Sergeant Major Canning, at their head. Knowing from past experience of the extreme reluctance of every member of his platoon to get up until the last possible moment, he looked upon their voluntary appearance on parade at that early hour as a compliment indeed. Percival stored his baggage in the luggage van, whilst he thanked his platoon and wished them luck. He then said his farewells to Ray and to the CSM before taking his seat in an empty compartment.

The small M & GNR locomotive gave a few warning snorts; then, tender-first, it began to draw its few carriages out under the road bridge. The adjutant and the CSM saluted, 11 Platoon presented arms, the notes of a plaintive farewell, played by the company piper, floated over the still-sleeping town. The junior subaltern's part in the defence of Norfolk was suddenly all over.

As the small train rattled along past so many familiar landmarks on the first stage of his long journey north, he wondered when next he might see Norfolk again. Certainly not for a long while. Perhaps not until after the war. Perhaps never. It had been his home for two years; he had come to know it and its people well. He had at one time expected to have to fight on its soil, perhaps to die there. He and his few men had stood on Weybourne Hope, and the enemy had not come. 'He who would old England win, must at Weybourne Hope begin.' He and 11 Platoon had in their own small way helped to prove the truth of that ancient couplet.

However, in his assessment he had failed completely to take into account the strange workings of the War Office's collective mind. In his innocence he had assumed that since it was known that he was spending his embarkation leave at his home address in Glasgow, and that Glasgow was also to be his port of embarkation, then his draft assembly point would be in that proximity. But no. This was just too simple for the mechanics of war-time administration. When final orders reached him these stated that all members of Draft RBFWG – letters which were to become imprinted on his mind as firmly as they were stencilled on all his baggage – were to report to a new assembly area based at Gresham's School, Holt, Norfolk.

'Is your journey really necessary?' asked the poster above the ticket office window in Glasgow Queen Street station where he presented his travel warrant. He wondered if the War Office ever read its own pronouncements – an idle thought. It was therefore with a definite sense of anti-climax that, embarkation leave over, he alighted from the train at Holt, and shortly afterwards found himself once again in the familiar surroundings of the officers' mess in the sanitorium of Gresham's School, only a few miles distant from the RSF at Sheringham. The eight officers who made up Draft RBFWG had time on their hands, with little to do until their final movement order arrived. The other seven were actually eager to see the surrounding countryside which was, for them, unknown territory; but the junior subaltern was reluctant to join them in their explorations. He felt extremely embarrassed at the very idea of meeting those good friends who had so recently given him such a marvellous send-off from Sheringham, and who must now believe that he was on the high seas, destined for battle in foreign parts. So he remained firmly in the mess, not daring even to visit The Feathers, that favourite haunt of RSF officers.

Four days later orders came through. The members of RBFWG were to proceed to Glasgow and thence to Greenock for embarkation. Once again, in the early hours of a summer morning, the junior subaltern entrusted himself and his worldly goods to the dubious care of the M & GNR. This time no send off, no 11 Platoon, no piper. Just another thin mist heralding another sun-hot Norfolk day. After his recent experiences he assumed nothing about the future. It was not until about 18 hours later when, tired, dishevelled and grubby after a tedious railway journey, the officers of RBFWG had settled on their bunks in a cramped cabin of RMS Duchess of Atholl, anchored in the Clyde at The Tail of the Bank, that he considered it to be safe to conclude that this time it really was Norfolk, goodbye.

POSTSCRIPT

The expected German invasion never materialised. Weybourne Hope remained inviolate. Instead, almost exactly two years after the events mentioned in the last chapter of this book, the 11th RSF set forth to meet the enemy in Normandy. The battalion was in frequent action in France and in Holland, acquitting itself with great distinction. The cost, alas, was high; over 170 killed, over 600 wounded. Many medals were won for bravery in battle, including one DCM and four DSOs. By the end of the campaign, Monty's 'amateurs' had more than justified the words spoken by Lord Trenchard all those months before, when he had addressed 11 Platoon outside Rose Cottage in Weybourne, and had told them that there were no better soldiers than those of The Royal Scots Fusiliers.